A Quick Guide to

BEHAVIOUR MANAGEMENT IN THE EARLY YEARS

Education at SAGE

SAGE is a leading international publisher of journals, books, and electronic media for academic, educational, and professional markets.

Our education publishing includes:

- accessible and comprehensive texts for aspiring education professionals and practitioners looking to further their careers through continuing professional development

- inspirational advice and guidance for the classroom

- authoritative state of the art reference from the leading authors in the field

Find out more at: **www.sagepub.co.uk/education**

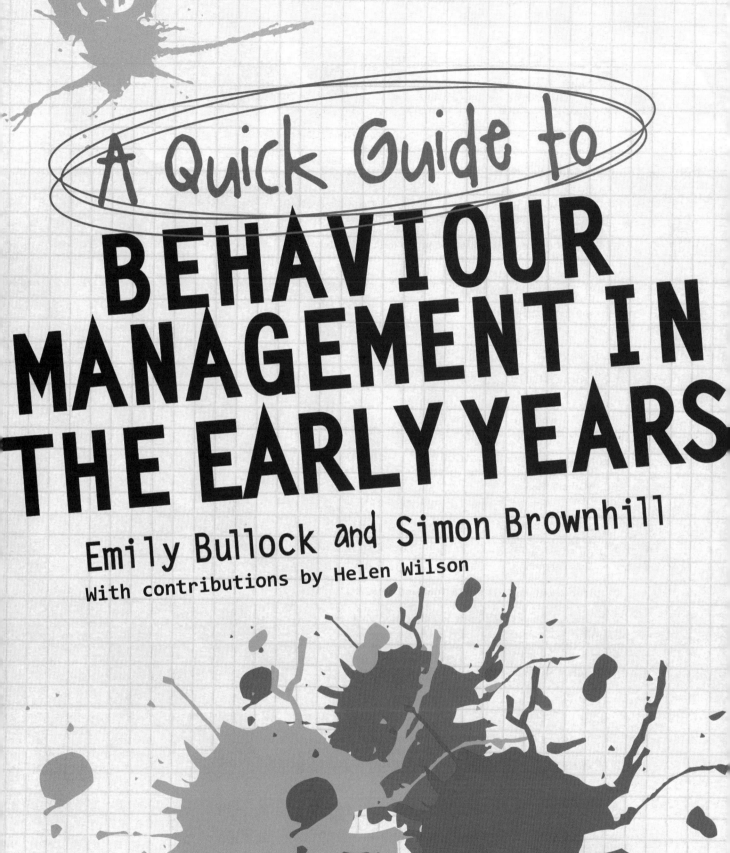

A Quick Guide to

BEHAVIOUR MANAGEMENT IN THE EARLY YEARS

Emily Bullock and Simon Brownhill

With contributions by Helen Wilson

⑤SAGE

Los Angeles | London | New Delhi
Singapore | Washington DC

First published 2011

SAGE Publications Ltd
1 Oliver's Yard
55 City Road
London EC1Y 1SP

SAGE Publications Inc.
2455 Teller Road
Thousand Oaks, California 91320

SAGE Publications India Pvt Ltd
B 1/I 1 Mohan Cooperative Industrial Area
Mathura Road
New Delhi 110 044

SAGE Publications Asia-Pacific Pte Ltd
33 Pekin Street #02-01
Far East Square
Singapore 048763

Library of Congress Control Number: 2011922833

British Library Cataloguing in Publication data

A catalogue record for this book is available from the British Library

ISBN 978-0-85702-164-9
ISBN 978-0-85702-165-6

Typeset by C&M Digitals (P) Ltd, Chennai, India
Printed by CPI Antony Rowe, Chippenham, Wiltshire
Printed on paper from sustainable resources

MIX
Paper from
responsible sources
FSC
www.fsc.org   FSC® C013604

Contents

For the most patient man I know – Marco

Emily Bullock

For Curtis Jnr, AKA 'Little Man'

Simon Brownhill

Acknowledgements

Emily and Simon would like to sincerely thank Helen Wilson for her contributions to the book.

Emily would like to thank the following people:

- Dad, Zoe Bullock, Marco Nocita, Tessa Moore and Karen Holt for the editing of her contributions to this book.
- Mum for her brilliant illustrations and hard work.
- Kev Fisher and Zoe Bullock for their stylish modelling.
- The Bullocks in general for being awesome.
- My brilliant friends in the UK, Hong Kong and New Zealand.

Simon would like to thank the following people:

- Mark Woodfield, Karen Fisher and Janet Goldsbrough for their fantastic editing of his contribution to this book.
- Dave Orwin for the making of many of the 'behavioural resources' seen in some of the photographs.
- Pete Ashford for some of the brilliant illustrations.
- Richard Richards for taking some of the wonderful photographs in this book.
- Amanda Gonsalves, Melissa Ramplin and Joanna Zurawska for their 'marvellous modelling'!
- My Mom, Pop and Sugarfluff for their continued love and support.
- My second family, my great friends, my work colleagues and the students I have the joy of working with at the University of Derby.

About the Authors

Emily Bullock BEd is a classroom teacher based in Hong Kong. She is currently teaching at Shatin Junior School, an International School run by the English Schools Foundation. Her teaching experiences span the 3–10 age range with a particular emphasis on the early years having spent the majority of her teaching years in Years 1 and 2. She is currently working on her MEd and is in the process of researching her independent study which will focus on creativity in the International Baccalaureate (IB) Primary Years Program. Emily has had experience of delivering guest lectures at the University of Derby for both BEd Primary Teaching and BA Education Studies with a focus on behaviour management, dance and teaching students with English as an Additional Language (EAL).

Dr Simon Brownhill is a Senior Lecturer in the School of Education at the University of Derby. He currently supports delivery on the Foundation Degree (arts) (FdA) Children and Young Peoples Services (CYPS) (Pathway), BA Education Studies and MA Education programmes, and has experience of working on the Initial Teaching Training (ITT) BEd and PGCE 3–7 and 5–11 provision. His teaching experiences span the 3–13 age phase with a particular emphasis on the early years (3–7) where he was formally an assistant head teacher of a large inner-city primary school. His research interests include men in education (the focus of his doctoral study), creativity in the classroom, children's physical development, developing children's reading skills, and supporting children from culturally diverse backgrounds. His infinite fascination with children's behaviour and its effective management has been the focus of both his undergraduate (BEd) and postgraduate (MEd) research projects, and of three collaborative/single-authored books on the topic.

Introduction

Behaviour: the 'current climate'

The management of children's behaviour continues to be a persistent area of concern in education today. It is essential to improve the behaviour of unruly children to maximize the learning which takes place in a setting. Behavioural issues can disrupt the flow of a lesson, affect the activities selected by practitioners and teachers, and can change the attitude of all involved. The impact of behaviour on practitioners'/teachers' abilities to thus effectively teach and ensure children actually learn can be significant, but behaviour *can* be managed through perseverance and a consistent, creative approach. This view is supported by Ofsted (2006: 1) who advocate that 'schools can reduce low-level disruptive behaviour in a reasonably short time, if everyone uses effective strategies'.

There is no doubt that good practitioners and teachers strive to maintain a harmonious working environment in which children can learn and teachers and practitioners can teach. The introduction of the Early Years Foundation Stage (DCSF, 2008a) and developments in primary school settings (see *The Primary Review*, DCSF, 2008b) have meant that there is a greater need for consistency in managing behaviour. Recent research indicates that practitioners and teachers who are studying for educational qualifications, and those in the infancy of their qualified roles, identify a need for effective management strategies. It is important that these strategies can be easily resourced and simple to use so that behavioural difficulties do not impact on standards within their setting.

This book is specifically designed to address this notion of 'effective strategies' by examining 100 practical resources which can be used by practitioners and teachers in both early years settings and Key Stage 1 classrooms to support the management of young children's behaviour between the ages of 0–8. The book will critically examine behaviour management within the long, medium and short term, considering strategies which can be used to manage behaviour as part of a behaviour policy, whilst supporting everyday practice in a setting. The resources offered are practical, 'hands-on' in their conception and application, and can be used to support practitioners and teachers in managing a wealth of different behaviours depending on the context and situation in which behaviours occur.

The book considers a wide range of physical, verbal, intellectual and visual resources for practitioners and teachers to choose from. These have been organized into 'themes', some of which include:

- tangible resources
- structures and systems

- quirky objects
- child-orientated resources
- rewarding good behaviour
- resources to manage sanctions.

This book is designed to support practitioners and teachers in selecting, adopting, adapting and reviewing behaviour management strategies which they use as part of their practice. While offering the reader a wealth of ideas, suggestions and tips, this book will allow the reader to engage in a critically reflective approach to behaviour management by supporting them in analysing, reflecting and modifying, where appropriate, the practice already established in their respective setting.

Why Another Book on Behaviour Management?

The driving force behind this book is our passion as collaboratively we have a good range of varied experience across the 0–8 sector. The book is written in response to demand and need. Students and staff need to feel well supported in their endeavours in the classroom setting and are always looking out for ways to effectively deal with behaviour. While we cannot claim that we have never had behavioural issues, our practice has been developed and refined through reflection, analysis, research, attending meetings and embracing continuing professional development opportunities. The book contains a collation of practice which we have read, used, tried, heard and tested. We are certainly not claiming that this book is 'the answer'; behaviour management is a continuous process of application, evaluation and reflection. It does, however, offer the reader a wealth of strategies that are designed to be selected from in order to manage behavioural issues that may arise.

This book is not designed to deal with the management of behaviours associated with special educational needs in detail; it does, however, offer strategies that can be applied to children in mainstream settings who have individual needs and exhibit various behavioural issues. Many of the strategies offered can be used by parents and carers at home with the support and guidance of practitioners and teachers; these are highlighted throughout the book. We consider this to be a supportive aspect of this book because we recognize that behaviour management is an issue with which parents and carers sometimes struggle. The direct relationship between behaviour and achievement is a concern for parents and carers; they recognize that if their child is behaving badly at school at the setting they are unlikely to be learning to their full potential. Practitioners and teachers, on the other hand, realize that if they are managing the behaviour of children who are disrupting sessions then the education of all children in the setting is at risk. The way to tackle both of these concerns is to focus on integrating effective behaviour management strategies into their 'suite of strategies' – this is where our book comes in!

It is important to consider why there are behavioural issues. Why do children misbehave? There are many reasons that can explain poor behaviour from children when in educational settings, some of which are listed opposite:

1. A lack of positive influence at home.
2. Issues at home that may include family problems, financial issues or ill health.
3. Media, an exposure to violent games, films and music.
4. A lack of male role models in the early years.
5. The feminization of teaching.
6. Peer influence.

Ofsted (2007) are very concerned about the behaviour in schools. It is suggested that peer influences particularly can lead to gang culture, and current societal influences are changing the ways in which children play, develop and behave. There are children as young as 8 years old being given ASBOs for antisocial behaviour. We believe that educational settings and schools should be seen as a safe place for children, and that a setting should not just be judged by the academic results and awards they achieve, but also by the way the children behave. We believe our book will support practitioners and teachers in offering this 'safe place'.

Theories of Behaviour Management

An important consideration in the management of children's behaviour is an appreciation of the relationship between theory and practice. Whilst our book serves to practically explore the concept and application of practical behaviour management strategies, we feel it is important at this point to highlight some of the theoretical perspectives which underpin quality provision in today's settings. These theories form part of our understanding and appreciation of behaviour management and have contributed to the information and strategies provided in this book.

Piaget

Piaget (1951) spoke of intellectual development. He suggested that children assimilate experiences, i.e. they fit new experiences and information into an existing schema. Piaget (1951) is of the belief that children learn through repetition and so in order to manage behaviour effectively, he believes that consistency is essential.

Vygotsky

Vygotsky (cited in Van der Veer et al., 1991) spoke of the 'Zone of Proximal Development'. He viewed the child as an apprentice that benefits from the accumulated experience of the culture by which he is surrounded. This theory suggests that a child will imitate others' behaviour, so in theory, by modelling positive behaviour and rewarding children who behave well, others will follow and they will then lead by example.

Skinner

Skinner (cited in Hardin, 2004) believed in 'behaviour modification'. When managing behaviour in settings, Skinner's positive reinforcement theory would come into play. This involves rewarding the children to reinforce positive behaviour using stickers and tangible rewards that encourage them to repeat the desired behaviour.

It is important to remember that behaviour management is not solely influenced by the thinking of theorists. Current thinkers offer innovation and new understanding to help practitioners and teachers gain an appreciation of how behaviour management 'works'. A select number of these current thinkers are offered below.

Sue Cowley

Cowley (2010) believes in a consistent and positive behaviour management style; listed below are her 'Be' points that she feels are essential to managing behaviour effectively:

- Be definite.
- Be aware.
- Be calm and consistent.
- Be positive.
- Be interested.
- Be flexible.
- Be persistent.

Paul Dix

Dix (2010) is keen to stress that the approach he has developed has been refined through classroom practice and experiences and not through theories. Dix suggests that the following points are 'key' to effective behaviour management:

- Communicate expectations clearly.
- Control your own emotions.
- Empathize with the students' needs.
- Be fair and consistent.
- Manage classroom issues.
- Reinforce positive behaviour rather than constantly dishing out sanctions.
- Build a relationship with the children you teach.

Simon Brownhill

Brownhill (in Shelton and Brownhill, 2008) proposed the 'Be Clear' approach. This approach to behaviour management follows three simple stages which allow practitioners and teachers to effectively address behavioural difficulties.

1. Be clear about what you see – do you know what behaviour you are observing? Can you define it?
2. Be clear about what's causing it – what factors are influencing this behaviour?

3. Be clear about what you are going to do about it – what strategies do you intend to put in place to manage the behaviour observed? Why have you selected these strategies?

How the Book Works

The book is organized into 10 distinct and purposely defined chapters:

Chapter 1 explores teachers'/practitioners' management strategies.
Chapter 2 focuses on teachers/practitioners and child management resources.
Chapter 3 encourages the reader to consider 'handy' behaviour management strategies.
Chapter 4 considers 'personal' behaviour management.
Chapter 5 offers ideas for creating behaviour resources that promote effective communication.
Chapter 6 concentrates on various structures and approaches to behaviour management.
Chapter 7 suggests 'timed' management strategies and resources.
Chapter 8 supports the reader in implementing influential management strategies.
Chapter 9 gives the reader a range of 'reflective' resources to consider.
Chapter 10 offers the reader a variety of ways to reward good behaviour.

The strategies are organized in this way to make the book easier for the reader to use. Each page has a similar layout with the content of each strategy offered in various sections. Each page offers the following standard information, which may vary slightly from one strategy to another:

*   Either a case study demonstrating how the strategy has been used in settings or an explanation of the strategy and how it is used.
*   A 'Handy Hints' box which will give advice and tips for making the most of the strategy in your setting.
*   Ways to adapt the strategy to make it work for you and the children in your setting.
*   A list of advantages, discussing why this is an effective strategy and the benefits of using it. You can use this section initially to see if the strategy is suitable for your particular needs.
*   Questions for consideration – questions that will support you in taking the strategy further and making it your own.
*   Links to similar resources in the book.
*   A photograph or an image has been included to provide a visual representation of each strategy. We decided that this would give the reader additional support when creating the resources.

The book has been designed to encourage you, the reader, to interact with the strategies. The questions for consideration, adaptations and behavioural monitoring templates are available to help you to choose the best possible strategies for the children in your setting. You should also consider rating the strategies as you work through them. In the back of the book, there is a page which allows for you to reflect on the effectiveness of the strategies by writing comments, recording any modifications you make and giving the strategies you have tried a score out of 10 (see page 121). It is important to continue changing and updating strategies in your setting so that behaviour management remains fresh and effective. If you decide to go back to a strategy, use the notes you made and the rating you awarded the strategy to determine if you would like to use it again.

Guidance and Advice

When selecting strategies to manage behavioural issues, you need to think about the context and situation in which you are applying a particular strategy. Put together a list of questions to help you to identify which *type* of strategy to use and then decide which of those would be most appropriate. If the behaviour management issue you have is with one specific child, consider photocopying one of the three blank behaviour observation sheets at the back of the book (see pages 117–19) to help you to pinpoint a focus area before choosing a strategy to implement.

 Case Study

Mr Hill was finding managing the behaviour in his Year 1 classroom a struggle and so after a recommendation from a friend he decided to purchase *A Quick Guide to Behaviour Management in the Early Years*. Mr Hill referred to the first chapter immediately as he felt that 'Management Strategies' was something that he could initially focus on. He read the strategy 'Your Voice' and carefully considered the 'Handy Hints'. He then went back to his classroom and made positive changes to the way he used his voice to manage children's behaviour. Mr Hill went back to the book after a week and turned to the effectiveness reflection sheet; he then gave the strategy a score of 9/10 and wrote down a few key points – 'My deep voice seems to grab the attention of the boys. Carrie seemed quite scared when I used this – suitable for girls?'.

We strongly believe that for this book to have the most impact, the implementation of the strategies offered within it should be consistent; in return, the practitioner/teacher will reap the benefit of the positive behaviours that these ideas will yield.

So go forth, tuck in, manage behaviour and enjoy working in a happier and more productive setting.

1

Teachers'/Practitioners' Management Strategies

Resource:	'Your Behaviour'

Explanation

'Do as I do, not as I say' is a phrase often used by adults. Children, as we know, mimic adult and peer behaviour which is why it is important that we model the behaviour that we want to see from the children in our settings. There are so many signals we give without even speaking; we tell children how we are feeling with our body language. If you present yourself in a way that suggests you are closed to interaction, a child is unlikely to respond to you in a positive way and may, in turn, present with poor behaviour.

You can also have a positive impact on the behaviour of the children in your class with your behaviour and how you present yourself. If you use eye contact with the children and concentrate on displaying encouraging and positive body language, children will feel more comfortable and safe and their behaviour will reflect this.

Case Study

Miss Chahal was having a terrible day; she had had a late night, could not find her keys as she left the house, and had a cold starting. She arrived at school feeling like she should have stayed in bed. The morning was awful – Miss Chahal found the children in her Year 1 class destructive, unreceptive and unfocused.

That afternoon, Miss Chahal decided to enter the classroom with an awareness of her body language, her manner with the children and her attitude. Being conscious about the way she was behaving, she found the rest of the day to be a much more pleasurable experience and the children to be far more manageable and tolerant. The classroom was a calmer, happier place to be and, as a result, the children were far more focused on their work and behavioural incidents were reduced significantly.

Handy Hints

- If a child is making you feel cross, turn away and count to 10. Approach the child with a calm voice and manner after 'your' brief time out.
- Keep a sweet treat in the classroom. When we need calories we can be more susceptible to losing our temper. This is a good quick fix!
- Leave your problems at the door – children should not be aware of any personal problems you may be having. It is not their fault and they should not be exposed to issues you have outside of the classroom.

Adaptations

You may need to modify the way you behave with the children depending on whether you are indoors or out. Try to maintain consistency in strategies you use wherever possible and the way you present yourself to the children.

If you are taking the children on a trip, make sure that expectations are made clear before leaving. The children are then prepared for the trip and your behaviour management strategies which may differ away from the setting.

Questions for Consideration

How can you make sure that you enter your setting with a clear mind? Try to think of something that you can do to calm you and clear your head in the morning. Here are some ideas: swimming, yoga, reading a book, coffee and a walk, or a chat with a friend or colleague.

Linked Resources

Your Voice – See page 11
Personal Mindset – See page 9
Humour – See page 14

Resource:	'Personal Mindset'

Explanation

Every practitioners'/teachers' mindset affects the way that they think about behaviour. If you are asked to think about the word 'behaviour' what examples of behaviour immediately come to mind? *Kicking? Swearing? Fidgeting? Laziness? Telling tales?* How many of you considered behaviours which we would *like* to see in children? *Politeness? Honesty? Sharing? Friendship? Turn taking?* If your mindset is negative then you are more likely to pick up on these behaviours in your setting; if your mindset is more positive then it is likely that you will not only promote these behaviours but will also use more positive strategies to reward children for their positive behaviour.

Handy Hints

- Avoid going into your setting each day thinking that the children you work with are going to be badly behaved – think positive!
- 'Look for the good' – make a point of highlighting to others the positive behaviours of children in your setting as and when they become apparent.
- *Believe* that the children you work with are well behaved and tell them this – encourage them to strive to meet your positive expectations.
- Say 'Positive! Positive!' five times before you start a session – you will be amazed at the effect it can have on your children and your teaching/practice.

Advantages

- This resource costs absolutely nothing!
- A positive mindset can make a *real* difference in your setting.
- Promoting a positive mindset in children can influence their behaviour and their academic work for the better.
- A positive mindset is good for your own personal health and well-being.
- Children respond well to teachers/practitioners who have a positive mindset.

Adaptations

Encourage older children to develop a positive personal mindset in relation to their behaviour and their academic work/achievements.

Verbalize your thoughts to children about your personal mindset so that they are aware of what you are thinking.

Support parents in helping them to develop a positive mindset when dealing with behavioural difficulties at home.

Questions for Consideration

How often do you go into your setting believing that you are not going to have any behavioural difficulties to deal with that day?

Which parents of children in your setting do you think would benefit from support in developing a positive mindset in response to their child's behaviour at home?

Linked Resources

Your Face – See page 13
Body Language – See page 10

Resource:	'Body Language'

Explanation

A powerful resource which you have your parents to thank for is your body; this can be used in a variety of ways to effectively manage children's behaviour in the setting. The way that you stand, the way that you sit, the way that you move around the children, and the way you 'hold' your body (slouched, upright, rigid, relaxed) elicits strong messages about who you are and what you expect in terms of the behaviours from the children you work with. Those of you who stand tall, use simple hand actions to gain attention (a click of the fingers; a clap of the hands; a wiggle of the fingers), and those of you who move with purpose and command will help to present a confident practitioner/teacher who expects good behaviour from their children.

Handy Hints

- Use different parts of your body to elicit different messages, e.g. a raised eyebrow for surprise; a warm smile for praise and acknowledgement of a positive behaviour.
- Avoid folding your arms – whilst this might be comfortable, it creates a 'barrier' between you and the children.
- When you sit on a chair, sit near the edge of the seat so that your back is away from the chair – this presents someone who is in control and ready.
- Moving closer to a child who is doing something inappropriate always has a positive effect; by doing this you step into their personal space and the child becomes uncomfortable, stopping whatever they are doing to see why you have come over to them. This will then have effectively stopped the inappropriate behaviour!

Advantages

- Using your body costs absolutely nothing (apart from the clothes that you have to wear to cover up your body!).
- Body language communicates about 60–70% of any message that is given by someone; it is a powerful way of sharing approval and concern over children's behaviour.
- Young children need to learn about non-verbal as well as verbal communication; using this strategy will help them with their development of 'reading' different forms of communication.

Adaptations

Think about your body posture, your gestures, your eye movements and your facial expressions – adapting these for different children will elicit a wealth of different messages for children to interpret and respond to.

Using verbal messages, e.g. commands, requests, questions and statements will add to the impact of your body language; consider adding these when you are using your practitioner/teacher 'glare'!

Questions for Consideration

How might you use body language to convey the message 'I think you are trying really hard'? What about 'I hope you are going to pick that toy off the ground'?

How might you say 'That was a very kind thing to do' without using speech?

Linked Resources

Your Face – See page 13
Your Behaviour – See page 8

Resource:	'Your Voice'

Explanation

The impact your voice has on a group of children is immeasurable. By using your voice as a management tool, you can affect the atmosphere in your setting. For maximum effectiveness, a practitioner/teacher should try to use and vary the following six elements of their voice: tone, pitch, rhythm, timbre, loudness and inflection. Children will become bored and will learn less with a teacher who does not modulate their voice.

It is important that you adapt your voice in order to guide and support children effectively. It should not however be assumed that your voice is only used to manage behaviour; your voice can also be used to encourage children. If a voice has quality and liveliness, children can be motivated to participate and learn; and a quiet calm voice can be used to settle the children if they are highly strung. By altering the tone of your voice in your setting, you can easily influence the attitude and mood of children. Your voice is an essential 'tool of your trade'.

Handy Hints

- Teachers should avoid raising their voices to manage behaviour; this can unsettle children and in the long term be ineffective.
- Bad behaviour can come from the improper use of a voice. Always consider the tone that you are using with the children.
- Your voice can also be used as a valuable reward strategy. By altering the tone of your voice, you can positively reinforce good behaviour.
- Use your voice to give the children choice, not to assert power.
- Volume control – remember that if you use a loud voice, the children will copy.

Advantages

- It is a strategy that can be taken anywhere you and the children go.
- By using your voice in a positive, calm and assertive manner, you can remain calm and the children respond positively.
- The voice can be used in so many different ways to manage behaviour in your setting, e.g. through direction, explanation, praise, criticism, advice, support, maintaining interest and motivating the class.

Adaptations

You can adapt this strategy for older children by accompanying your voice with typed instructions, countdowns, and recognition of good behaviour by pre-recording messages for children and either e-mailing the messages or displaying them on an interactive whiteboard.

Use visual cues with your voice in SEN settings so that children are aware of how you are using your voice, if they are unable to hear or struggle to recognize the changes in tone.

Questions for Consideration

How could you support the children in using their own voices to manage problems with their peers?

Consider this... A child is found taking things from another child's bag. Practise the tone you would use in this instance and what you would say to the child.

Linked Resources

Your Face – See page 13
Your Behaviour – See page 8

Resource:	'Positive Praise' (Helen Wilson)

Explanation

This is the cheapest and one of the most effective resources available to you for promoting positive behaviour in young children. Most children respond well to praise and encouragement and this strategy, if used well, is very powerful in promoting positive behaviour. If you use praise effectively and appropriately, children are much more likely to demonstrate positive behaviour. On the other hand, if a child displays negative behaviour and you ignore the behaviour and concentrate on positive things that they have done, they are far more likely to repeat the positive behaviour than the inappropriate behaviour. By using clear, concise and specific words that clearly voice your approval, the child is more likely to model the behaviour you want to see.

Handy Hints

- Make sure praise is 'sincere'.
- Remember to praise the action not the child! For example, say 'That was a very kind thing that you did picking Sam's coat up' rather than 'Oh, you are good!'
- Use 'You' Messages instead of 'I' Messages; when praising a child, say, 'You did that all by yourself' instead of saying, 'I like the way you did that'. A 'you' message teaches children to have pride in themselves and to own their actions, ensuring they focus on what they can do for themselves.
- It's important not to give praise that focuses on the end product, but that instead focuses on the effort the child has made throughout the process.

Advantages

- Praising the child for trying their best to accomplish tasks gives them incentive and drive to continue to strive for the best that they can be. It also teaches the children to feel proud of themselves.
- It is a totally free resource that we can all use in our settings.
- It makes you, the practitioner, feel good, as well as the child.

Adaptations

If a child is demonstrating unwanted behaviour, praise a child nearby who is demonstrating a positive behaviour. The shift of focus of your attention will often result in a positive change in the behaviour of the child who is misbehaving.

Change from focusing on the negative behaviour to celebrating the positive by actively praising children – you will see a difference!

Questions for Consideration

How often do you praise a child in comparison to identifying negative behaviours?

Are you aware of all the ways you can praise effectively?

Linked Resources

Your Behaviour – See page 8
Teaching Assistants – See page 41
Midday Supervisors – See page 43

Resource:	'Your Face'

Explanation

You can say a thousand words without speaking and often non-verbal communication can be more effective than words, especially with young children. It is important that you use your face to encourage, warn, support and engage the children in your setting. It is equally important that you have control of your expressions and are aware of the emotions you are conveying to the children.

By using expression, you can send signals that help to reinforce positive behaviour. This is not only an effective strategy to manage behaviour, it is also a mode of communication that improves the relationship between practitioner/teacher and child by allowing non-verbal understanding.

Eye contact is a vital form of communication – practitioners/teachers who make eye contact open the flow of communication and convey interest, concern, warmth and credibility.

Handy Hints

- Children in your setting who speak EAL (English as an Additional Language) rely heavily on your facial expressions to 'read' a situation. With these children, you may want to over-emphasize and simplify instructions to support their understanding.
- Use lots of face cream! As a teacher, you will be using your face more so than in other professions (bar actors), and you want to try to prevent those crow's feet for as long as you can.
- Stand in front of a mirror and practise facial expressions you use in the class to warn, discipline and praise children. Do you think that you clearly convey the emotion you are trying to?
- Remember that facial expressions are related to emotions and so can quite often be involuntary – try to remember this. It is important that you are in control of your expressions.

Advantages

- By using facial expressions, you can protect your voice which can easily become strained and over worked in an educational setting.
- By using your face instead of your voice you can maintain a quieter, calmer setting.
- This is a strategy that needs no resourcing and can be very effective.
- The children learn to read your facial expressions and will respond more quickly to them the more you use them.
- Smiling is a vital form of non-verbal communication that transmits happiness, approval, warmth, friendliness and affiliation.

Examples of Emotions that Can Be Conveyed Through Facial Expressions

- Anger
- Confusion
- Excitement
- Happiness
- Sadness
- Pride
- Contempt
- Frustration
- Surprise
- Worry
- Disappointment

Questions for Consideration

Next time a child in your setting disturbs teaching with low-level disruptive behaviour, how would you manage this – using your voice as little as possible?

What do you look like when you are trying to warn and praise a child?

Linked Resources

Your Voice – See page 11
Your Behaviour – See page 8
Body Language – See page 10

Resource:	'Humour'

Case Study

The children in Miss MacFarlane's class were finding phonics very dull. They were bored with learning the same old phonemes and no matter how she tried to 'dress it up', the children knew they were repeating work that they had done before.

Miss MacFarlane had an idea – she set up the phonics activity as normal but told the children that depending on the score they got, they would play forfeits. If they managed to identify all the sounds correctly and spell the words she called out, then she would have to carry out a forfeit; if not then the whole class would have to carry out the forfeit. The children won (of course!) so Miss MacFarlane stood by her word and danced the Macarena much to the children's delight. Humour can be used to enhance children's experiences in subjects they might otherwise find challenging or boring. If a child enjoys a lesson, they are more likely to approach the same subject with a more positive attitude next time. When children enjoy learning, they will present better behaviour and are also more likely to retain what they learn and be able to reapply it in subsequent lessons.

Handy Hints

- By laughing at yourself and encouraging children to do the same you create a friendly environment that facilitates learning.
- Give the children ownership of forfeits by offering choices.
- Remember not to use the children as the point of humour unless they initiate it, as this can be damaging.
- Only use humour at appropriate times.
- Make sure that you can 'pull the children back' – the last thing you want is the class out of control and unable to do their activities.
- Make sure the humour is not too advanced for the children – irony or sarcasm is not appropriate for younger children or children with SEN.

Advantages

- The children are motivated to learn.
- They will enjoy activities and lessons more.
- It is fun for you to teach and rewarding to see the children enjoying themselves.
- It takes fewer muscles to smile than it does to frown. If you're not careful working with children can create wrinkles!
- Children are less likely to misbehave if they are happy and engaged in their learning.

Adaptations

In nursery settings, you could use puppets to praise children who are making good choices and showing positive behaviour. You could also ask a member of staff to dress up in a costume and praise children who are behaving well.

With older children, you can use more sophisticated humour such as irony. However, it is important that you do not ridicule the children.

Questions for Consideration

Do you think that humour is a preventative form of behaviour management? Can it be used to tackle incidents?

How could you use humour to model good behaviour without ridiculing the children?

Linked Resources

Your Voice – See page 11
Your Face – See page 13

Resource:	'Clothing'

Explanation

The clothing that you wear in your work setting says a lot about who you are as a human being and as a professional – those of you who 'power dress' by wearing suits emphasize traits such as organization, strength and control; those of you who adopt a more 'casual' attire convey a more relaxed and easy-going disposition. The clothes that you wear for work every day give out both implicit and explicit messages about how you feel, how you teach and how you expect children to behave in your setting; the colour, style and presentation of your clothing can have a real impact on the behaviours that children in your setting exhibit.

Handy Hints

- Avoid clothing with derogatory phrases or quirky sayings which children might be able to read and misinterpret.
- Ensure that the clothing you wear is clean and freshly laundered – young children are not afraid to tell you when your clothing is dirty or 'smelly'!
- Wear clothing which allows you to move freely and represents your personality; bright and colourful clothing suggests to the children someone who is happy and confident and caring; dark, dull colours suggest someone who is strict, unapproachable and unsympathetic.
- Ascertain whether there is a written or an 'unwritten' policy about the kinds of clothing that you should wear in your setting – do parents, carers and students know about this when they come to support you and the children?

Advantages

- From the moment children see your clothing, they instantly pick up on 'whether you mean business' or not; clothing has an immediate impact on behaviour.
- The way you dress impacts on the kinds of behaviours you will experience in the setting.
- If you want to change children's behaviour overnight, consider changing your outfit – it really works!

Adaptations

Due to the nature of practice in early years settings, a casual attitude towards clothing helps to replicate the relaxed and 'free flow' approach to learning and teaching in these learning environments.

For practitioners/teachers working with older children, smart clothing such as shirts, blouses, jumpers and ties help to emphasize a firm attitude towards positive learning, teaching and behaviour.

Questions for Consideration

What messages do you think your clothing gives to children about you as a person and you as a professional?

How might you change your clothing to emphasize a stronger position on positive behaviour in your setting?

Linked Resources

Your Face – See page 13
Personal Mindset – See page 9

Resource:	'Displays'

Explanation

The displays that you have in your setting can be a useful resource to manage children's behaviour. The focus of the display, the colours used to create the display, and what is actually displayed on the board can influence the behaviours of the children you work with. We have found that children are likely to demonstrate positive behaviours, in terms of developing a sense of pride in their environment and building up collaborative behaviours, when they have a say in what the focus of the display is, the colours which are used to back the board and mount the work, and whose work is displayed on the board. Let children make collaborative decisions about the displays in your setting and you will be amazed at how much they care about their displays and the positive behaviours this yields.

Handy Hints

- Displays can have an area of learning (early years) or subject focus (primary) or can be designed to promote positive behaviours, e.g. sticker charts, children's names on the 'Sun' and 'Cloud', or the 'Kindness Tree'.
- Think about when it would be a good time to change the displays in your setting so that they continue to have a positive effect on the children you work with.
- Support children in mounting and labelling their work; let them make the decisions as to how it is arranged on the display (after all, it is their work!).
- Strive to ensure that every child has made some contribution to each display so that they feel valued.

Advantages

- Displays are a very visual way of exhibiting the achievements of children in the setting, both in terms of their behaviours and in terms of their learning.
- Children will develop a vested interest in their environment if they are allowed to make decisions about how their working environment is going to look.
- Using displays to track the positive behaviours of children in the setting promotes healthy competition and a keenness to behave well.

Adaptations

Use displays to respond to the needs and interests of the children, e.g. a space theme for boys (each time they are noted as behaving well, their 'spaceship' moves one step closer to reaching the moon) or a princess display for the girls (each time they are noted as behaving well, the princess has another jewel added to her tiara).

For older children, encourage them to write and present the labels which accompany the work on the displays so that others are informed of what the learning is around the work displayed.

Questions for Consideration

Which display board in your setting is currently in need of being changed? What could it be changed to to display and promote positive behaviours in your setting?

What opportunities are there for you to get the children you work with to collaborate on a display?

Linked Resources

SMARTC Target Board – See page 53
Behaviour Targets – See page 55

Resource:	'Special Helper Role'

Explanation

Children love responsibility; it helps them feel valued and important. In your setting, do you find that children are always asking if they can help you in some way? They want to please you, help you, to be acknowledged.

By naming the children as special helpers, you can ensure that one or two children every day are being recognized for work or behaviour from the previous day by being assigned the title of 'Special Helper'. These children can take registers, sharpen pencils, hand out books, etc. – the list of jobs you assign to the special helpers can be appropriate to you and your setting. For the whole day, they are exclusively responsible for the set of jobs you have assigned to them and for ensuring that they complete these tasks.

Handy Hints

- Give the 'Special Helpers' chairs to sit on – this will make them feel even more valued and give their responsibilities more importance.
- Make the special helpers a badge that they can wear so that everyone knows they have been chosen to be the 'Special Helper'.
- Put up a list of responsibilities – use photographs/pictures if the children struggle to read the list so that they know what is expected of them for their day.
- Make a certificate or personalized sticker for the children to wear or take home so parents and carers are aware that they were chosen to be the 'Special Helper' that day.

Advantages

- Children will not be asking to help you all the time as they know only the 'Special Helpers' can do the jobs.
- It saves you and your support staff time by ensuring that small jobs are taken care of by the children.
- The children have ownership of the jobs, they are responsible and, in turn, develop a level of independence.
- The roles provide classroom routine which ensure the children know what to expect from day to day.

Adaptations

This strategy could be adapted for older children by allowing them to develop and enforce a set of 'promises' with clear rewards and sanctions that the children could be made responsible for.

Younger children can be given the role of 'Teacher Helper'. They might be called upon throughout the day to complete tasks alongside the teacher rather than follow a list.

Questions for Consideration

What roles would you assign to the children in your setting?

How can you ensure that the children are completing the jobs?

Linked Resources

Peer Mediators – See page 44
Setting Routines – See page 63

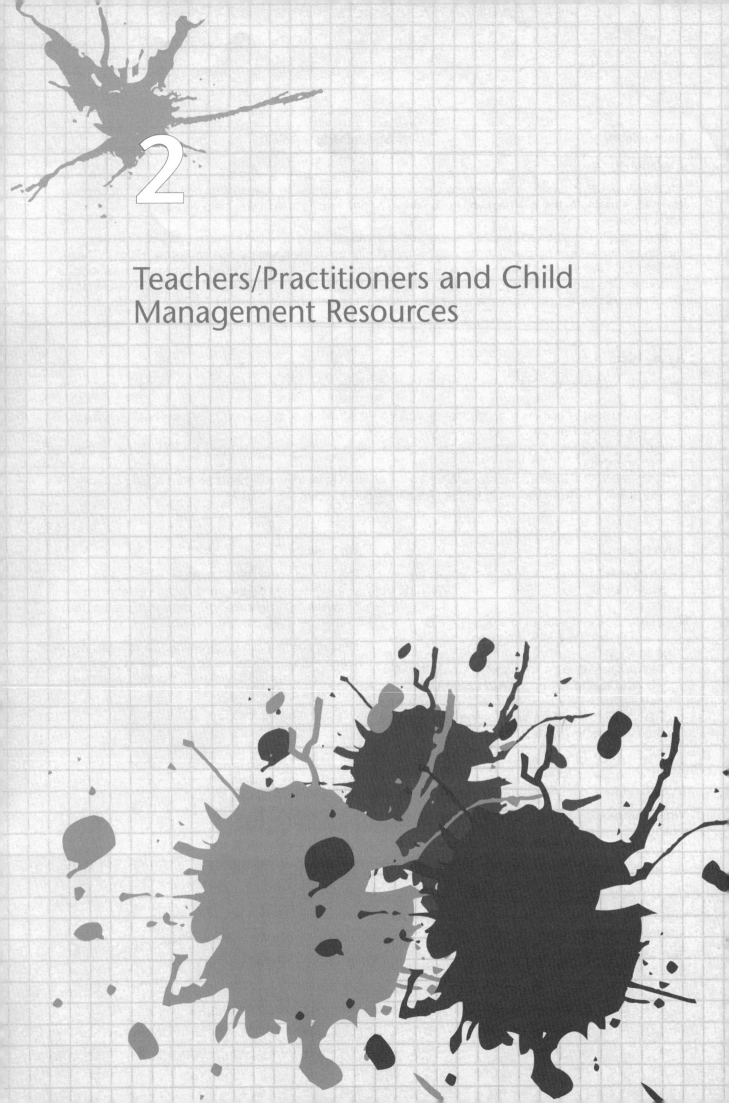

2

Teachers/Practitioners and Child Management Resources

Resource:	'Masks'

Explanation

Masks are a really fun way to support the children in managing their behaviour. They can be used in several ways to reduce behavioural issues in your setting:

1. When you would normally give children verbal warnings or instructions, you could use a variety of masks in a way to prompt the children. For example, one mask may mean there is too much noise; by wearing the mask it acts as a reminder for the children to use inside voices.
2. The children can use the masks with drama to work through behavioural issues.
3. The masks can be used by children to share feelings and emotions. By hiding their face, they may be more comfortable to talk.

Handy Hints

- If you have a collection of masks, allow the children to decide on what each mask could be used for.
- Put the masks within reach of the children with a picture or statement reminding them why you might be using that mask so that the children have visual support.
- If you are using the masks to make sure the children are comfortable to share their feelings, do not pressure them to share or they may become uncomfortable and be reluctant to talk.
- Do not mix the three ideas in one setting at the same time; it might confuse the children.
- Keep the masks fresh, you may want to rotate the ones that you are using every half term.

Advantages

- The masks are a fun and very visual prompt to support the children in what they need to do.
- Children need to be observant to see when you put a mask on.
- The children are able to explore their own understanding of their behaviour with peers.
- Children develop speaking and listening skills.
- Children have a way to express their emotions while feeling less vulnerable.
- Even if the children do not want to talk, putting the masks on in a quiet space may be therapeutic for them.

Adaptations

Rather than buying masks which can become quite expensive, why not have a class competition and involve the children in designing the masks?

Allow the children to interact with the masks; they can do some role play as you the practitioner/teacher which will reinforce the meaning of the masks.

Set up a quiet area with masks and allow the children to go in as they choose. This space can be used for children to play with friends or reflect on their own.

Questions for Consideration

Would you use prompt cards for the children who were using the masks for drama? What would they say?

How could you ensure the children can access the masks when they need to?

Linked Resources

Hats – See page 21
Clothing – See page 15
Role Play – See page 65

Resource:	'Puppets' (Helen Wilson)

Explanation

Puppets come in a whole variety of shapes, forms and sizes, from a gorilla to a friendly granddad. Puppets are a very versatile resource. They can work especially well with younger children and can provide an excellent way for children to recognize and explore positive and negative behaviour and its effect on others. They can be used successfully to work through targeted behaviours and even be used to mirror some positive behaviour that you wish to promote. Puppets can be used to work through potentially difficult situations like starting in a new class or introducing a new topic or focus for discussion. A puppet used correctly can become an 'ambassador' for positive behaviour!

Handy Hints

- Be careful in your choice of puppet – some children are easily scared! Introduce the puppet slowly to the children. Allow the children to bond with the puppet.
- Think about the puppet as a person. Look at it while it is talking to you and ensure it looks at the children when they are talking – don't ever talk to the puppet when it is not on your hand.
- Keep the movement of the puppet as natural as possible; it doesn't have to be constantly moving. Use gentle movements not jerky ones.
- Practise first so that you are comfortable with using and talking to the puppet in character; open the mouth for every syllable.

Advantages

- Children often become far more vocal and animated when a puppet is around, even encouraging the shyest child to speak.
- Puppets help to engage the class in a topic or problem that needs resolving.
- The puppet can be a confidant for the children. It can be used to ask questions about concerns they may have.
- They can be used to explore issues from a safe viewpoint.

Adaptations

Think about using a 'themed' puppet to introduce particular topics, for example a 'friendly faced' puppet when looking at settling in a new class.

Not all puppets have to speak! If you are not confident, get the puppet to whisper to you while you talk to the children for the puppet.

A puppet is a great prop to use in story telling to bring stories to life.

Questions for Consideration

Do you feel that all children would engage well with a puppet?

Do you feel that your confidence in using the puppet may affect the impact of the puppet?

Consider the length of time you would use the puppet for different-aged children and particular topics.

Linked Resources

Masks – See page 19
Hats – See page 21

Resource:	'Hats'

Explanation

The use of hats to manage behaviour is a very simple and fun strategy. Depending on the setting, hats can be used for lots of different reasons; in a classroom, a teacher might put on a particular hat which the children know means they need to stop working and talking. In a nursery, a practitioner might put on a hat that the children will associate with tidying up their activities and moving to the carpet. Different hats can be used to let children know how you, the practitioner, is feeling about what is happening in the setting. Hats can also be used to give instructions and offer praise, you could even use the hats to instigate routines in the classroom. When the children become familiar with the hats, they will recognize different hats as an indication, for example, to wash their hands in preparation for lunch or for any other daily routines.

Handy Hints

- You could allow the children to choose what the hats are for; this will give the children some ownership of the strategy.
- The hats might become a little repetitive. You could encourage other colleagues to use the same strategy and change the hats within the setting to keep the impact fresh.
- It would be effective if the children had the opportunity to role play/interact with the hats.
- Could you have a daily hat selector who is in charge of collecting the hat they think you should be wearing depending on the situation?
- You should be able to pick up some very cheap hats from charity shops, so expand your collection without breaking the bank.

Advantages

- The children are quickly able to identify with each of the hats and their meaning.
- The hats bring humour to behaviour management.
- It is a non-gender specific form of classroom management, and all children can identify with it.
- The children can use the hats in role play and reinforce their understanding of what each hat means.
- You can involve the children in helping to run this strategy.
- There is no need to use your voice – you can rest it with this strategy.

Adaptations

You could use masks in place of hats to manage behaviour.

Select the hats of characters the children may know, e.g. Fireman Sam, Postman Pat, Bob the Builder. Work these hats into the strategy.

Allow the children to bring hats in from home if they wish for 'guest' behaviour hats. These hats could manage seasonal behaviour issues.

Questions for Consideration

If you were going on an educational trip and you could only take one hat, which hat would you choose?

How might you encourage parents to use a similar approach with children at home?

Linked Resources

Humour – See page 14
Traffic Lights – See page 102
Setting Routines – See page 63

Resource:	'Magic Carpet'

Explanation

The magic carpet is one of the most effective resources we have used in our own classes in relation to behaviour management. The magic carpet is a versatile resource which can be used in a number of ways, either to reward children for their good behaviour, or to manage the behaviour of children who are behaving inappropriately. For the children who are well behaved in class, the practitioner/teacher can roll out the magic carpet and take the children on an imaginary ride as a thank you for their brilliant behaviour. For those children whose inappropriate behaviour needs to be addressed, the magic carpet can be brought out and used as a clear space where the children can sit and reflect on their behaviour with the practitioner/teacher.

Handy Hints

- Make a clear decision as to whether you want to use the magic carpet as a *reward* for children or as a way of *managing* the behaviour of children who are behaving inappropriately. Once you have made your decision then stick with this, otherwise the children will become confused as to what the magic carpet is actually for.
- If the children struggle to come up with an idea as to where they would like to go on their imaginary ride, ensure you have already thought of some places yourself, e.g. space, a cereal bowl, the South Pole, Elmer the elephant's forest, down a plug hole, inside a DVD player, in a washing machine, over the Sahara desert.
- Maintain the pretence of the magic carpet being special by only bringing it out when necessary.

Advantages

- Children respond extremely well to the magic carpet, particularly if practitioners/teachers 'sell' the premise of the carpet to their children – we have known children to squeal with delight when they know they are going on an imaginary ride!
- If used infrequently, the magic carpet can be a special reward for exceptional behaviour.
- For those children whose inappropriate behaviour needs managing, practitioners/teachers can help these children to believe that their behaviour will improve by the 'magic powers' of the carpet.

Adaptations

The magic carpet could be a magic *drape*, a magic *rug*, a magic *blanket*, a magic *bench*, a magic *throw*, a magic *mat* or a magic *duvet cover*.

The magic carpet can be used to reward good behaviour or manage undesirable behaviour, depending on the needs of the children.

The magic carpet can be used for a few weeks with your children or be used as a long-term strategy.

Questions for Consideration

Would you use the magic carpet to reward children for their good behaviour in your class/setting or manage their undesirable behaviours?

Consider the amount of space you have in your class/setting – would you use the magic carpet indoors or outdoors?

Linked Resources

Circle Time – See page 75
Rest Mats – See page 99

Resource:	'Pictures and Posters' (Helen Wilson)

Explanation

Children can learn through a variety of different media, of which pictures and posters are one form. When children see a picture or poster, they often know immediately what it represents – they provide an effective visual prompt. Seeing an image is a much more potent way of teaching than just telling. Pictures and posters, which are often very bright and colourful, act as a concrete reminder of behavioural expectations, for example what good manners are, or the routine to follow when washing your hands. Whatever message is needed, educational posters are a fun and colourful way of getting it across to the children in your setting.

Handy Hints

- Colour is used to warn people of hot/cold and stop/go. The same colours can be used in educational posters for similar reasons. Posters that are meant to warn of danger are often red or black. Yellow is often meant to present something fun and happy. Choose your colours carefully to ensure effective communication.
- Posters or pictures can be scaled down to handy A4-sized flash cards which can be used at circle time, in play areas (sand/water tray) or in small group activities to remind or prompt children about behavioural expectations.
- You could also reduce the size to A5 and use the pictures as reminders of behavioural expectations that are being targeted for individual children.
- Small copies of the cards or posters can also be used as a reward. When a child is observed displaying the positive behaviour, a small copy of the picture can be given as a reward. A grid could be included under the picture to record how many times the desired behaviour is observed.

Advantages

- Although text can be used, there is no need to include it.
- Posters and pictures are a fun and attractive way of getting key messages about behaviour across to all children regardless of their levels of literacy.
- Using posters as a prompt helps the practitioner/ teacher as they do not have to keep repeating information.

Adaptations

Colour is an important feature of educational posters. The use of colour makes a poster both eye-catching and informative, helping the student to understand whether the behaviour pictured is desired or not.

Children can make their own posters or pictures to remind them of routines, for example the hygiene routine after using the toilet.

Make a poster/picture with a range of desirable behaviours displayed with an arrow or binoculars pointing to the focus of the day/week.

Questions for Consideration

How do you use posters to promote key messages?

When would you involve the children in making and designing their own posters or pictures, as part of golden time or playtime?

How often do you change the posters in your school/ setting?

Linked Resources

Displays – See page 16
SMARTC Target Board – See page 53
Learning Targets – See page 57

Resource:	'Stories' (Helen Wilson)

Explanation

Stories are the most fantastic resource we can use with children in managing behaviour. Stories help children to make sense of themselves and their world. Stories are a way of introducing children to new vocabulary, places, experiences, behaviours and concepts they may never normally meet. Stories can not only be read from books in the form of tales, myths, fairy tales, legends and fables, but can also be used very powerfully in oral telling. Stories offer so many opportunities to develop richness in language and learning but they are also fundamental in developing a sense of identity. Stories offer the ability to experience and explore a whole range of emotions, behaviours and experiences within a 'safe framework'. The beauty of a story is that it can be paused or stopped, it can be closed and re-opened at any time.

Handy Hints

- Create a regular time for story telling and make it a magical activity.
- Use a wide range of stories and story-telling techniques to bring the content to life.
- Don't overuse questions and pauses in story telling as it can result in the overall message being 'lost'.
- Use props, puppets and actions in story telling.
- Your voice is the best resource in story telling – use tone, pitch, pace and volume to enhance the story.
- Include oral stories and stories from different cultures to act as starting points for discussion on behaviour and behavioural expectations!

Advantages

- Stories are a free resource – you can access libraries to add to a resource bank.
- Stories do not require any special space or equipment – you can tell them any time, any place and anywhere.
- They are very powerful, as the behaviour and experiences being read about are concerning a character in a book, not a particular individual within the group who may be displaying the negative behaviour.

Adaptations

Create a magic 'story-telling chair' or wear a magic 'story-telling cape' to make the story more powerful.

Get other adults in to tell stories so children have a range of voices and story-telling styles to listen to.

Get adults from a range of different cultures to share their stories.

Stop telling the story at a crucial point and get the children to guess what happens next.

Questions for Consideration

Why and how do you use stories at present?

Have you checked your book stock to make sure it includes stories about behavioural issues?

How many different story tellers have you used?

Linked Resources

Puppets – See page 20
Magic Carpet – See page 22

Resource:	'Music'

Explanation

Music is amazing. It creates a mood, sets an atmosphere and can be motivating. There has been lots of discussion about the type of music that should be used in educational settings. It is often assumed that classical music is the most effective for creating a calm environment. This is not strictly true, as children respond in different ways to different music but if a child recognizes a piece of music, they will respond to having music as a reward and will behave accordingly to continue to receive that reward.

Music can be used at different times during the school day, not necessarily only when the children are working.

Handy Hints

- Give the children the chance to choose the music as a reward for good behaviour. This will give the children ownership of the reward and will also motivate the children to show sensible behaviour.
- Specific music can be used to provide the children with a routine, for example, music that prompts the children to line up or tidy up their classroom or work areas.
- Set up an area in the setting that you can use for quiet work with music using headphones. This may be as part of a reward or to support children who are catching up with their work.
- Do not play the music too loud or the children may try to compete with the volume – keep it quiet and remind the children that if they cannot hear it then they need to be using quieter voices.

Advantages

- The children enjoy listening to music.
- You can expose children to different genres of music.
- Children develop an appreciation of music and may become more aware of rhythm and timing.
- It is enjoyable to have music playing while *you* work.
- The children will work quietly when music is playing so that they can enjoy it which can result in a calmer classroom.

Adaptations

Older children could use Mp3 players to listen to their own music while they work independently. This gives the children responsibility and also minimizes disruptive chatter. Ensure the volume is appropriate or fixed on the Mp3 players as young children's ears can be damaged by listening to music that is too loud.

In a PVI setting, the children could have access to the music player so that they can choose the music that they listen to as a reward.

Questions for Consideration

Would you use music with a child who was upset or angry? What type of music would you use?

How would you find out the musical preferences of the children in your setting?

Linked Resources

Music Sessions – See page 66
Setting Routines – See page 63

Resource:	'Distraction Devices'

Explanation

Many children find it difficult to sit and concentrate during whole-class work, for varying reasons. Some children may have English as a second language or suffer from Attention Deficit Disorder. The type of issues that may arise during whole-class teaching can include; fidgeting, poking or touching other children, pulling/damaging items of clothing and making noises. The children who are presenting with this behaviour are often doing so because they are unable to sit quietly and listen. This does not mean the child is 'naughty'. Many adults (myself included) find it a challenge to listen for extended periods, and it is even more challenging for young children. These children simply need a means to keep themselves occupied so that they are able to focus on what is being said by any adult leading sessions.

Depending on the type of learners the children in your class are, they could find being told to sit quietly and listen very challenging. Kinaesthetic learners particularly find carpet time a challenge. By allowing children to use distraction devices, kinaesthetic learners are more likely to engage and retain knowledge and understanding.

Handy Hints

The distraction device can be anything that you think the child will respond to. Here are a few ideas if you are struggling for inspiration:

- Blu-Tack® balls
- stress toys
- Chinese worry balls (without the bells!)
- silly putty
- playdough
- a small soft ball.

Another handy hint for minimizing the need for distraction devices is to teach with a VAK (visual, auditory and kinaesthetic) approach wherever possible, to engage and stimulate all learners. See this strategy for more advice.

Advantages

- Group work can be more fluid with less interruption.
- The children with the distraction device are able to re-focus their attention.
- Children feel supported and are able to concentrate, so experience more success and less pressure and stress.
- Other children in the class are not distracted by potentially disruptive behaviour.

Adaptations

Younger children in PVI settings may all benefit from using distraction devices – the younger a child is, the shorter their attention span. If you have a box of objects available, you could ask a member of support staff to be involved in distributing as they see fit.

Children with fine motor skill problems may also benefit from having a distraction device that can develop more precise control. Using these devices during listening time will support their progress.

Questions for Consideration

Who do you think would benefit from a distraction device in your setting?

What different objects would be appropriate for use in your settings?

Linked Resources

Setting Routines – See page 63
Learning Styles – See page 86

Resource:	'Designated Carpet Spaces'

Explanation

Virtually all settings/classrooms have a carpet area for the children to sit on – usually this is used to bring all of the children together for whole-class teaching, circle time opportunities or story time. There are always those children, however, who cannot 'stay put' on the carpet and we are sure you have seen children 'wriggling' around the carpet to try and sit next to their friend. Carpet squares are an effective way of keeping children 'in their space' by assigning them to either a carpet tile, a marker on the carpet or an 'offcut' carpet square positioned near to the practitioner/teacher. These can be used at the start of term, at the start of the week or at the start of each session/lesson – *it is your choice!*

Handy Hints

- Ensure each child is given a specific space to sit, clarify where this is with each individual so that the children do not get confused or become uncertain as to where they should be sitting.
- Strive to mark out carpet spaces using different colours, different shapes or different markers so that each space is different from the others (where possible/appropriate).
- Work with the children to decide where *they* would like to sit – can they justify why they should next to their friend? Clarify what will happen if they abuse this privilege.

Advantages

- Children who find it difficult to stay in one place on the carpet have a clear space to sit in – it is easy to see if they have moved away from their space as their mat/space will be empty!
- This is a relatively cheap and easy idea to deploy – many classes/settings now have 'Mat Monitors' who arrange the mats on the carpet area in the morning and clear them away before the end of the day, thus promoting positive and responsible behaviours in the classroom.
- Children like to know *where* they should be!

Adaptations

Use offcuts from carpets – ask the parents/carers of your children if they are having any new carpets put down in their house. One setting we know uses handkerchiefs as their markers which the children have decorated themselves.

For younger children, you could put down small plastic hoops that they can sit inside.

For older children, demark their space with a sticky label on the floor or encourage the children to bring a teddy or a toy which 'sits' in their space when they are away from the carpet area.

Questions for Consideration

Which children in your setting would benefit from a designated carpet space?

What resource would be best to help this child/these children from wriggling around the carpet area?

Linked Resources

Magic Carpet – See page 22
Behaviour Dust – See page 39

Resource:	'Parachutes' (Helen Wilson)

Explanation

Play parachutes are circular, nylon, coloured fabric of different diameters that children hold around the edge and use to play team games. The games that are centred on moving the parachute in a variety of different ways are engineered to encourage co-operative, non-competitive play and reinforce turn-taking and sharing. Parachute games also help to strengthen upper body muscles, mainly the muscles in the shoulders, arms, hands, and the larger body; they can also help to refine gross motor skills. Parachute games can be used to build on all areas of development in children.

Handy Hints

- The parachute can be used both indoors (in a large space!) and outdoors and can be linked into a reward system, for example by rewarding positive group behaviour or as a chosen favourite activity.
- Set very clear rules and boundaries about behaviour before play starts, as the children tend to get quite carried away at first!
- Have the children remove their shoes before approaching the parachute if they are using it indoors.
- Encourage the children to space themselves around the parachute so that there are no large gaps. If there is a large gap, you may ask specific children to invite friends from other classes to join you as a reward.
- Have the children hold the parachute with both hands at all times.

Advantages

- Parachute games encourage co-operation between all children within the class.
- It is not necessarily a skills-based activity, so any child at any level can be fully involved with the activity.
- Language and number concepts can also be incorporated into most parachute games; it is a great way to introduce prepositions and the vocabulary linked with directionality.

Adaptations

Other items like beanbags and balls can be added to widen the activities. The idea is to try and keep the ball moving without letting it fall off the parachute.

A wide variety of different games can be played for different ages and abilities; the parachute is popular with very young and older children.

You can create a secret hiding space by raising the parachute up then tucking it behind you and sitting on the edge; this creates a fantastic story or poetry telling space!

Incorporate songs, rhymes, and movement activities into the parachute time.

Questions for Consideration

Have you and your staff considered the balance of non-competitive games as well as competitive games that your children engage in? Consider the benefits of both.

Do you tend to save such activities as special treats or do you allow the children to choose them as a reward for positive behaviour?

Linked Resources

Outdoor Area – See page 64
Physical Games – See page 89

3

'Handy' Behaviour
Management Strategies

Resource:	'Behaviour Binoculars'

Explanation

'Behaviour Binoculars' are simply a set of binoculars (these could be real binoculars, a set of toy binoculars or a pair made out of a cardboard tube and a piece of string) which 'look out' for good behaviour in children. The practitioner/teacher is encouraged to wear them around their neck throughout the day and look through them, either to 'spot' a child who is behaving well on their own or within a group context. This is an excellent resource for managing the behaviour of children both inside and outside; 'Behaviour Binoculars' can also be used to develop observational behaviours as practitioners/teachers can encourage children to look for birds, specific colours and different types of trees or interesting cloud formations.

Handy Hints

- Use the behaviour binoculars during children's learning experiences, both indoors and outdoors.
- Make a point of 'looking' for children who are being well behaved as opposed to those who are behaving inappropriately.
- As opposed to verbally acknowledging your use of the binoculars, simply raise them to your eyes – children quickly learn that you are looking for good behaviour once you have explained their use to them.
- Make the binoculars 'distinct' so that they are different to other binoculars in the setting by decorating them, painting them or accessorizing the strap.

Advantages

- Children react very quickly when practitioners/teachers bring the binoculars to their eyes – this can help to eradicate inappropriate behaviours with speed and efficiency.
- Behaviour binoculars are a cheap and easy resource to make and use in the setting.
- Support staff and parents can also be encouraged to use behaviour binoculars in the setting and at home with support.

Adaptations

For older children, practitioners/teachers could use a monocle or a large magnifying glass (think Sherlock Holmes!).

For those practitioners/teachers who would like to keep a record of which children they spot being well behaved, their names could be recorded on a large pair of laminated binocular lenses displayed on a board in the setting.

Questions for Consideration

When would be an appropriate time to introduce this resource to the children in your setting – the start of term? The end of a week? Why?

Should the children be involved in the decorating of the behaviour binoculars? If so, why? If not, why not?

Linked Resources

Make-Me-Smile Board – See page 101
Wow Card – See page 34

Resource:	'Whistle or Bell' (Helen Wilson)

Explanation

The use of a whistle or bell is a very effective way of getting everyone's attention. You can use either the whistle or the bell as a signal for stopping or starting an event or activity very quickly. A short blast on a whistle or sound of a ringing bell easily cuts through a noisy environment and can be used as a very effective signal of event/activity change, especially in an outdoor environment.

Handy Hints

- Make sure all of the children know and understand the significance of the signal.
- Do not overuse the whistle/bell. Sound the bell or whistle for a short time and then wait for the desired effect using praise to reinforce the children displaying the desired behaviours.
- Always use the same signal – for example, one short use of the whistle means stop what you are doing, while two short whistles signal carry on.

Advantages

- The bell and whistle are both very simple and effective tools that don't require the use of a loud voice to get attention.
- They can be used in a variety of environments to signal a change in expectation of behaviour.
- They can be used gently in a more enclosed environment to bring attention to something positive.

Adaptations

Get the children to devise the signals so they have more ownership of the strategy.

As a reward, allow one of the children to be in control of the signal.

Use the signals at the start of an activity as well as at the end of an activity, especially if it is 'fun', so the signal is not always attributed with stopping an activity.

A quietly chimed bell could be used to signal a particular session – for example, a story or music session or to signal a particular event, behaviour or activity that has been performed with a desirable outcome.

Questions for Consideration

Is there a right and a wrong time/place to use a piercing whistle or bell?

Does the sound of a whistle or bell upset anyone working in your setting?

Linked Resources

Midday Supervisors – See page 43
Outdoor Area – See page 64

Resource:	'10cm Ruler'

Explanation

The 10cm ruler is really a metaphor for helping to manage the noise levels children make, either when they are inside the classroom/setting or outside in the play area/playground. Some children have a tendency to shout and scream or talk loudly – the 10cm ruler allows practitioners/teachers to gently ask children to lower their voice by using their '10cm voice', i.e. one which is quiet and calm. To support children in understanding what this means, practitioners/teachers can model the modulation in their voice by talking quietly or indicating 10cms on a ruler. Consider how children would change their voice if they were asked to use their '30cm voice'? *Put your fingers in your ears for that one!*

Handy Hints

- Actively model what you mean by a '10cm voice' so that the children understand what you expect in response to this polite request.
- Clearly indicate 10cm on a ruler using paint, coloured paper or an arrow so that it is visually clear for children to see where 10cms appear on the ruler.
- Indicate on the ruler where you think that the children's voices were when you asked them to use their 10cm voice – show them how this has changed as they lower the volume of their voices by sliding your finger/a cardboard arrow down the ruler.

Advantages

- This is a very quick and easy way to get children to lower the volume of their voice.
- For children who are very 'visual' in their learning, having an actual ruler is a power indicator of the volume their voice was at and how this changes when they lower it.
- For many children, showing them the ruler instantly has an effect on the volume of their voice as they recognize that they were being too loud.

Adaptations

Younger children and those who have special educational needs may not understand the concept of centimetres. Practitioners/teachers could use linking cubes as a visual aid so that children are encouraged to use their 'little tower' voice as opposed to their 'skyscraper' voice.

For older children, it is useful to use a large ruler as a visual aid as opposed to a small ruler as the larger ruler will have more visual impact for the whole class.

Questions for Consideration

Do you think it would be better to have your 10cm ruler visual aid displayed on a display board or kept in your pocket? Why do you think this?

Which particular children do you work with would respond positively to using this resource to manage their loud voice?

Linked Resources

Noise-O-Meter – See page 104
Whistle or Bell – See page 31

Resource:	'Referee Cards'

Explanation

Referee cards are one of the simplest and most effective strategies we have used in the settings we have worked in. The cards work in a similar way to those used by referees who oversee football matches – the practitioner/teacher has about their person two cards, one of them is green and the other is red. When they see a child behaving in an appropriate and sensible way in the setting/classroom, the practitioner/teacher will show the child the green card as an indication that their behaviour is 'good'. If the child is shown a red card, this indicates that the child is currently doing something which displeases the practitioner/teacher; this should highlight to the child that they need to stop whatever it is which the practitioner/teacher is unhappy about seeing. Once this happens, the practitioner/teacher should show the child the green card to indicate that they made the right choice in behaving appropriately.

Handy Hints

- Some practitioners may consider the red card to be rather 'severe', especially when you consider that in football a player would be sent off the pitch; are you prepared to send children out of your class if you show them a red card? Consider changing the colour of the red card to yellow.
- For whole-class teaching opportunities, prepare a larger set of referee cards for the children to see.
- Ensure that your teaching assistant/colleagues have a set of referee cards themselves so that they can use them with groups of children, thus reinforcing the use of these cards as a consistent strategy in your setting.
- Use facial expressions to accompany the displaying of the different cards to reinforce the message, e.g. a smiling face with the green card and a surprised/frowning facial expression when you have to use your red/yellow card.

Advantages

- This resource provides an instant visual indication as to whether a child's behaviour is good or 'not so good'.
- The cards are relatively easy to carry around and use in any context, e.g. indoors, outdoors, hall, corridors.
- Boys respond positively to this idea due to its links to football.
- The cards are simple to make and can be used by any adult working with children, e.g. teachers, practitioners, parent helpers, teaching assistants, student teachers/practitioners.

Adaptations

Consider changing the colour of the red card to yellow *unless* you are prepared to send children out of your class.

For older children, it is useful for them to discuss with you what behaviours will result in a green and a red card being given; consider devising a chart so that when the children are shown a card they can record its colour on the chart – what will happen when children receive five green cards in a row?

Questions for Consideration

What would you give a red card to children for in your class? What about a green card?

How often would you give a red card out in your class each day?

How will the children know which behaviours will yield a green or red response from you?

Linked Resources

Traffic Lights – See page 102
Numbered Cards – See page 37

Resource:	'Wow Card'

Explanation

This is a simple strategy that can be used to manage low-level disruptive behaviour without interrupting activities or whole-class input. The idea is that a series of cards, one green, one red and one with 'Wow' written on it are used as a non-verbal, visual support to encourage children to take responsibility for managing their own behaviour.

The practitioner/teacher uses the set of cards as a management tool during teaching time or whole-class work. When used as intended, they will allow sessions to continue to run without disruption.

If children are displaying low-level disruptive behaviours such as talking to friends, bothering other children or calling out, the cards can be shown as a series of warnings. The green card is to let children know that they are showing good behaviour, the red card is shown if the children are disrupting sessions. The 'Wow Card', which is the most fantastic thing for any child to see, is shown to let a child know that they are displaying outstanding behaviour.

Handy Hints

- Consider using the cards in different ways to make the resource more flexible. They could be put on a chain that can be worn around your neck, they could be used as flash cards, or as enlarged versions that you can place photographs of the children onto.
- Put a child in charge of the 'Wow Card' so that sometimes they can show others that they recognize good choices.
- Make some stickers saying 'Ask me why I got shown the "Wow Card" today' so the children are able to share their achievements with their parents.
- Make sure you use the green card as much as the warning card, to reinforce positive behaviour.

Advantages

- The 'Wow Card' recognizes the children who make good choices the whole time.
- This is an easy resource to make that can be used in a variety of settings and can be easily adapted.
- It is a quick visual tool that can be used without disrupting teaching to support children in managing their own behaviour.
- The children will feel very special if they are shown the 'Wow Card'.

Adaptations

For younger children, the 'Wow Card' could be converted to stickers so that others are able to see the children who have made good choices throughout the day.

The effectiveness of this strategy may be short-lived for older children. To ensure the children are still motivated by the cards, encouragement can be given by sending e-mails to the children/parents of children who are shown the 'Wow Card'. Another worthwhile strategy could be to allow the children to re-name the 'Wow Card' with a name they prefer.

Questions for Consideration

How could you use the 'Wow Card' with a larger group of children, for example in an assembly or outdoor play setting?

Do you think that the 'Wow Card' would be more effective for an individual child, a small group or for a whole class/group of children?

Linked Resources

Referee Cards – See page 33
Stop and Go Cards – See page 35
Traffic Lights – See page 102

Resource:	'Stop and Go Cards'

Explanation

'Stop and Go Cards' are a very simple management tool. One card is green showing the word 'Go' on one side and is plain green on the other and the other card is red showing the word 'Stop' on one side and is plain red on the other. These cards can be used to start and stop children during activities and can also be used to prevent bad behaviour. The children need to recognize the importance of the cards and to immediately stop what they are doing and face the practitioner/teacher or begin/continue with a task when shown the cards. The red side of the stop card can also be used in whole-class teaching and can be shown to particular children who are making the wrong choices to manage behaviour. The green side of the go card can be used in a similar way to show recognition of positive behaviour.

The cards can also be used outside of the classroom to manage behaviour, for example during PE lessons and assembly time, and could easily be used on trips away from your setting.

Handy Hints

- Make the cards large enough for the children to be able to see.
- Choose a child who has impressed you with their behaviour to be in control of a reduced size set of the cards that they can wear around their neck. Involve this child in choosing when to use the cards alongside you.
- Perhaps use a flashlight or try saying 'Stop' or 'Go' with the stop or go card if the children struggle to notice.
- The cards can be used as part of a wider reward scheme, for example if the children are shown the go cards as a reward then you may award them a sticker or a house point.

Advantages

- The cards can be an excellent way to manage low-level disruptions.
- During whole-class buddy chatting, the cards are very effective in controlling the length of discussion.
- The cards can resolve behavioural problems quickly before they get out of hand.
- The cards can be used to praise positive behaviour and warn children who are showing poor behaviour.
- The children easily associate stop and go with the colours of the cards.

Adaptations

In an open-plan setting, the stop and go cards could be simultaneously flashed onto multiple interactive whiteboards. In this large version, they could also initiate tidying away.

A coloured light could be used instead of the cards for older children, or perhaps even a gesture or action.

The cards can be used for many reasons; to manage noise, to prevent low-level disruptions, to initiate or end an activity, or to praise children.

Questions for Consideration

Can you think of a situation in your setting where the stop and go cards might be particularly effective?

What noise could you use to accompany the cards in a busy situation?

Linked Resources

Referee Cards – See page 33
Traffic Lights – See page 102

Resource:	'Stamps' (Helen Wilson)

Explanation

Using an ink stamp is an easy and very effective way to encourage and reward positive behaviour in our early years settings/classrooms. They are an instant response to reward and recognize positive behaviour. You can use a stamp on a piece of work, a chart or even on the back of a child's hand. Stamps can be used to encourage particular positive behaviours in individual children which can in turn have a positive effect on the behaviour of other children. By rewarding and reinforcing positive behaviour, you are likely to witness repetition of the desired behaviour. Using stamps can also help build confidence and self-esteem in the child in a particular subject or topic area.

Handy Hints

- Make sure that the type of stamp used appeals to the individual child. Find out about their interests so the stamp has real appeal; for example, a smiley face stamp might not be received with as much delight as a dinosaur.
- Display the stamps on a chart so there is an audience for the achievement – a stamp on a page in a book is often forgotten.
- Focus on one behaviour at a time so the child is clear on which positive behaviour you are looking for.
- Make sure all adults are clear on which positive behaviour is being targeted or rewarded.
- Don't over-use them or they may lose their impact.

Advantages

- This provides a very easy and immediate reward system.
- If used consistently and carefully, the stamps can result in very positive behaviour changes quickly.
- There is a large variety of stamps and ink colours to choose from, from cartoon characters to favourite storybook characters.
- Stamps are easily transferable to home so parents can be involved too!

Adaptations

Stickers are also a very useful and effective alternative to stamps.

Create a chart to display how many stamps are collected.

Use different ink colours for different desired behaviours.

Use a target number of stamps to aim for a special treat!

Stamps can also be used to reward behaviours such as concentration, helpfulness, tidying up.

Questions for Consideration

Would stamps work as rewards for all children? You must really get to know what works for individual children in order to achieve a change in behaviour.

Linked Resources

Positive Praise – See page 12
Stickers – See page 52
Reward Charts – See page 110

Resource:	'Numbered Cards'

Explanation

Numbered cards are a very simple and easy resource to make and use with children to manage their behaviour, both indoors and outdoors. The practitioner/teacher has about their person a number of cards, some with the number 1 on them, some with the number 2. As the children are playing/working, the practitioner/teacher will give a child who is behaving particularly well a card with the number 1 on – this child must then go and post it in a box marked '1'; for those children who are not behaving well, the practitioner/teacher will give these children a number 2 card which needs to be posted in the '2' box. At the end of the session/day, the practitioner/teacher counts out the number of cards in each box – *have more 1s been given out?* If there have been more 2s issued, the practitioner/teacher can ask the children what this means about the behaviour throughout the session/day.

Handy Hints

- Ensure that the cards are different colours (green for 1s and yellow for 2s); ensure that the boxes that the children post the cards into are the same colour as the respective cards.
- Avoid making a 'big thing' about giving the card to the child – place it near to them with a smile (1s) or a surprised look/slight disappointment (2s) so that it does not interfere with their learning, particularly those who receive a 1 card.
- Regularly review the meaning of the 1 and 2 cards with the children as a whole group and individually so that they are clear as to what behaviours they will get each card for.
- Keep a written log of the cards that you give out so that each child is given a card during the session/day.

Advantages

- Young children like to know that they are behaving well – they will quickly get used to wanting and working hard for a 1 card.
- Peer influence helps to manage the behaviours of those children who receive a 2 card – we have seen children helping those who have had a 2 card to think about their behaviour and what they could do to get a 1 card.

Adaptations

The age of the children determines the number of cards used – young children should only be given 1 and 2 cards; with older children you could extend this to numbers 3 and 4 if you feel this is appropriate.

The numbers on the cards could relate to specific behaviours, depending on the age and abilities of the children, e.g. 1 = positive *manners*; 2 = positive *working behaviours*; 3 = positive *relationships with peers and adults*.

The numbers could be changed for letters or words, e.g. A and B; *Positive! Think! Well done! Reflect!*

Questions for Consideration

Which colours do you intend to make your cards out of? Why have you chosen these?

If a child gets a 1 card, can they get *another* 1 card in the day? What would you do if a child in your setting gets three 2 cards in a row?

Linked Resources

Referee Cards – See page 33
Stop and Go Cards – See page 35

Resource:	'Raffle Tickets'

Explanation

The idea behind raffle tickets is that the children earn the tickets as a kind of token. On any occasion the child does something particularly kind or special, if they produce pleasing work or demonstrate good behaviour, they are given a ticket. The tickets can be given by any adult in a setting. After receiving a ticket, the child's name is written on the back and the ticket is put into a box in the setting. What happens next depends on how you want to reward the children – this can be done in a number of ways. I would recommend for younger children that the draw is done weekly or even daily but for older children a draw could be done every 2 weeks or even at the end of a half term. The reward could be; a small prize, a certificate, an activity for one child or a reward for a group of children whose tickets are drawn, for example, extra play or a small party.

Handy Hints

- Advertise the prize before the draw to motivate the children.
- Make a feature of the raffle ticket box – you could ask the children to decorate the box in the first week in the setting.
- Invite a member of the senior management team to the draw.
- You could send a letter home for the children that are recognized so parents are aware that their good behaviour/hard work has been acknowledged.
- For every draw, remember that there are lots of children who earned tickets that will not be mentioned. Congratulate the whole class before carrying out the draw.

Advantages

- The children receive instant recognition with the raffle ticket.
- The scheme is easy to apply across a whole setting rather than in one class or unit.
- The draw is something all children will look forward to every week/day.
- The strategy will remain effective as you can keep it exciting by changing the rewards regularly.

Adaptations

Involve older children in the planning of the rewards. Allow them to create posters to advertise the weekly prize. Encourage the children to collate the tickets and do the draw for the rest of the class.

Rather than using numbered raffle tickets for the younger children, use small laminated photographs of the children or cards with their names on so that they can be more involved in the draw and have a better understanding of the tokens.

Questions for Consideration

Would you acknowledge the children who had a significant number of tickets in the box at the end of a week even if they did not win the final prize? How?

Could you involve the children in the draw? How?

Linked Resources

House Points/Table Points – See page 112
End of Term/Year Awards Assembly – See page 81

Resource:	'Behaviour Dust'

Explanation

Behavioural dust is a versatile resource which can be adapted and used in any situation with any children of any age, both at home and in the setting. The dust can be used at any time, either to address behavioural issues or to pre-empt behavioural issues and stop them before they start. The dust only works when practitioners/teachers sprinkle their children with 'behaviour dust' at the start of the session/lesson to make the children 'well behaved'; if there are individuals who are behaving inappropriately then practitioners/teachers can speak to the child/children and sprinkle behaviour dust over them which will encourage them to make better choices regarding the behaviours they exhibit.

Handy Hints

- The behaviour dust can be *imaginary* or it can be *real* – consider using fine glitter or very soft coloured powder (we have found that no dust works best!).
- Behaviour dust can be kept in the practitioner's/teacher's pocket or in a special bag; always have it to hand!
- The dust can be sprinkled over the head of the child or over a particular part of their body, e.g. their hands or their feet, which is not behaving appropriately (they might be exhibiting punching or kicking behaviours which need to be managed).
- To maintain the idea of the behaviour dust having 'magical powers', ensure that only practitioners/teachers administer it.

Advantages

- Young children really 'buy in' to the idea of the dust being magical; use your story-telling skills to present the mystical and powerful effect that the dust can have on children's behaviour.
- This resource can be very cheap (i.e. it could cost nothing) or it can be very expensive if you use lots of dust on the children!
- The dust can be used on individuals, groups of children or the whole class, depending on the situation and the behaviours being exhibited.

Adaptations

Older children can be encouraged to rub the behaviour dust over a part of their own body which they recognize as misbehaving, e.g. their lips and mouth (if they use inappropriate words); their fingers (if they constantly fiddle with things).

Behaviour dust can be 'distributed' using a black and white magic wand for the boys or a pink sparkly star wand for girls.

Children can create their own container for their own behaviour dust if they wish to manage the behaviour of their peers.

Questions for Consideration

Who would the behaviour dust work best on in your setting?

Would you use imaginary or real dust? Why?

How often do you think you would use the dust with your class over one day? Why this amount?

Linked Resource

Whistle or Bell – See page 31

4

Personal Behaviour Management

Resource:	'Teaching Assistants'

Explanation

Teaching assistants are a very important resource in the management of children's behaviour. Having a consistent approach between the lead practitioner/teacher and the teaching assistant in terms of the ways desirable behaviours are rewarded and undesirable behaviours are dealt with is likely to result in a harmonious and productive working environment where children can learn, explore and be safe. Teaching assistants who observe and model the strategies used by the lead practitioner/teacher in the setting help to reinforce a strong and effective way of managing behaviour; this is likely to build productive and lasting relationships with the children.

Handy Hints

- Ensure your teaching assistant has access to a copy of the setting's/school's behaviour policy – give them time to read and reflect on its content.
- Talk with your teaching assistant about strategies you intend to use with your children – is your teaching assistant happy with the proposed strategies? Do they have any better suggestions? Can they spot any difficulties with the strategies being put in place?
- Collaborate with your teaching assistant when reviewing the successes or weaknesses of strategies used in the setting – do they have any good 'alternatives' to use with the children?
- Make sure that you purchase/make a second set of practical behaviour resources (see Chapter 3) so that your teaching assistant has their own version to use with the children they work with.

Advantages

- Collaborating with teaching assistants makes them feel part of the team.
- A consistent approach helps to prevent behavioural difficulties from escalating.
- Teaching assistants can be full of useful ideas – tap into their knowledge and expertise to get new ideas and to make them feel valued.
- When children know that the adults in the setting are 'singing from the same song sheet', this prevents them from exploiting one particular adult in the setting.

Adaptations

For younger children, teaching assistants need to share and discuss their behaviour management strategy needs with lead practitioners/teachers so that they can effectively manage any difficulties they experience with the children.

For older children, teaching assistants need to see the rules and the strategies used in class displayed and modelled as they may only be in class for an hour at a time.

Questions for Consideration

How might you be able to use your teaching assistant more effectively to manage the children's behaviour in your setting?

Does your teaching assistant have their own set of practical resources that you use to manage children's behaviour? If not, why not?

Linked Resources

Learning Mentors – See page 42
Parents/Carers – See page 47

Resource:	'Learning Mentors' (Helen Wilson)

Explanation

Learning mentors are a relatively new way of supporting children with behavioural issues. They provide the 'bridge' between academic practitioner/teacher support and the more pastoral support that is available in some settings/schools, to break down barriers to learning that some children may face. All learning mentors usually (although not always) are appointed from within the setting as it is vital that they have a sound knowledge of the children (and their backgrounds) that they are supporting. They should *not* be based in one class as their role is to support children when needed throughout the setting. Their role is to intervene and work with a child or group of children that are presenting behaviours that are disruptive or behaviours that causes concern; they remove them from the classroom and, through discussion, trace back the root cause of the particular behaviour, investigating the reasons for the behaviour and discussing the child's concerns, fears and anxieties in order to find how best to move forward and restore positive behavioural patterns.

Handy Hints

- Do not see learning mentors as extra playground support – their role is far more valuable.
- It is vital that learning mentors are given a base to work from where children can feel 'safe' in discussing personal issues freely; the space should be secure, calming, quiet and permanent.
- Use display, posters and pictures to reinforce positive behavioural messages in the learning mentor room.
- Include a 'games' area to help promote positive behaviours like sharing, turn taking and respect for equipment and the environment.
- Get the children to name the learning mentor's space so that they have 'ownership' of the space.
- Find out what other schools in your area use learning mentors and set up a support group.

Advantages

- You have someone on site, on call, to refer children with varying needs who are struggling in the classroom or during playtimes.
- 'Learning Mentors' can work alongside the teacher to help children achieve their full potential.
- The use of a 'Learning Mentor' allows the teacher to return to teaching the class, knowing that the problem behaviour is being managed.

Adaptations

Older children within the school can be used as a type of 'Learning Mentor' to support younger children in some areas, for example reading or playground issues.

Have drop-in 'Learning Mentor' sessions at lunch- and breaktimes so issues can be dealt with immediately.

Questions for Consideration

Do you have the support of the whole staff in making this positive support mechanism work?

Do you have a space that can be used solely by 'Learning Mentors'?

Are there schools nearby that have 'Learning Mentors' that you could visit and set up a network of support with?

Linked Resources

Teaching Assistants – See page 41
Peer Mediators – See page 44
School Council – See page 45

Resource:	'Midday Supervisors'

Explanation

Midday supervisors have to manage children's behaviour during one of the most difficult times in the day – lunchtime! The daily hurly-burly of children rushing into the dinner hall to eat their lunch and then race out onto the playground/play area again presents midday supervisors with many different situations where they have to manage undesirable behaviour, e.g. running, shouting and rudeness. Midday supervisors are not trained practitioners and many of them do not have any knowledge of the strategies which will help them to successfully address all of the behavioural issues which present themselves during the dinner hour. Working in collaboration with your midday supervisor, however, can have a positive impact on the behaviour of your children; this can be achieved through embracing some of the Handy Hints which are offered below.

Handy Hints

- Talk to your children about their use of manners and respect to all adults who work in their setting/school.
- Offer midday supervisors a list of simple strategies they could use to manage children's behaviour during lunchtime, e.g. time out; the midday supervisor 'glare'; stickers; verbal praise; lowering their voice; and logging incidents in a small book and following this up with the class practitioner/teacher at an appropriate time.
- Encourage your midday supervisor to come in and work in your setting/class so that they can build up positive relationships with the children they are going to look after – learning the children's names is half the battle!
- Regularly thank midday supervisors for their efforts – they are more likely to stay 'on side' if they feel valued.

Advantages

- Effective midday supervisors help to ensure that you can maximize learning and teaching time after lunch as opposed to having to deal with behavioural difficulties when the children come back into the setting/classroom.
- Midday supervisors can reinforce expectations and support children who have exhibited undesirable behaviours with you in the morning.
- Children are happier when they are cared for by people who they know and who are able to manage others effectively.

Adaptations

Midday supervisors with younger children are in a better position to manage their behaviours as they are usually assigned smaller groups to support when eating, toileting, making transitions from the classroom to the dinner hall, and finally to the playground/play area.

Offer training sessions for midday supervisors on managing children's behaviour – this helps to assure a level of consistency.

Questions for Consideration

Does your midday supervisor know all of your children's names?

What 'quick fire' strategies could you share with your midday supervisor to ensure their time with your children is calm, supportive and 'behaviour-less'!

Linked Resources

Raffle Tickets – See page 38
Thinking Chair – See page 97

Resource:	'Peer Mediators'

Case Study

Marco and Tessa were watching the children playing when they noticed an argument by the swings; they walked over and introduced themselves, reminding the children that they are peer mediators and that they do not take sides. Marco encouraged the children to share their version of what had happened; he remembered he needed to listen carefully to both sides of the story and so gave both sides the chance to explain what had happened. Marco then listed the obvious problems that had caused the conflict for the children involved. Tessa supported the children and encouraged them to come to an agreement and then both mediators worked with the children as they carried out the agreement.

    After the incident, Marco and Tessa recorded the names of the children who they worked with on the playground in the peer mediator's book which the practitioner/teacher checked at the end of the week.

Handy Hints

- Refer to websites to support you with the implementation of the programme (www.peermediation.org/).
- Appoint children as Peer Mediators as a reward for being good role models for other children.
- Give the children caps so that children on the playground can easily identify them and approach them if they need support.
- Check the incidents in the book regularly to see if the same names appear; if they do, perhaps concentrate on managing the behaviour of these children to minimize incidents.
- Rotate peer mediators every half term so other children have the opportunity to develop valuable skills.
- Make sure you support the children, teach them how to be a good mediator and be available to them when they are on duty.

Advantages

- The children are given responsibility and feel respected and valued.
- Midday supervisors have support on the playground in managing incidents.
- Children learn valuable social skills as well as how to manage any conflict they might experience.
- Playground/outdoor issues are more quickly resolved.
- After outdoor play, the children will settle quickly rather than wanting to tell tales.

Adaptations

It is far less likely that there will be incidences indoors as there is more structure. If issues do arise, allow the children to be involved in mediating any indoor conflict.

Younger children may find aspects of peer mediation difficult to manage, so use a midday supervisor to shadow the children, if possible, so they can be supported in managing the incidents.

Allow the children to write a playground code to support the peer mediators in managing incidents.

Questions for Consideration

How would you train and support the peer mediators?

What resources do you think the children would need to be effective peer mediators?

How many peer mediators would you use at any one time?

Linked Resources

Midday Supervisors – See page 43
School Council – See page 45

Resource:	'School Council' (Helen Wilson)

Explanation

A School Council is a group of representatives, elected by their peer group to raise key issues with Senior Managers and Governors within the school. The School Council can also propose and take forward ideas for new initiatives and projects on behalf of their peers, for example: types of resources provided for playtime, friendship benches or the types of after school activity clubs on offer.

School councils meet at regular intervals during term time, with an adult to support them in managing the meetings and guiding them to action their decisions.

Handy Hints

- Make the purpose and aim of the School Council very clear to everyone.
- Have regular feedback sessions for the other children so that they see their ideas and opinions are being acted upon.
- Make sure that when ideas are not acted on, the decision-making process is explained so the reason behind the decision is clear.
- Change the representatives on a regular basis so that all children can have the opportunity, if desired, to take their group's ideas forward.
- Make the roles and responsibilities of the representatives very clear so that children elect representatives that they feel will fulfil the role well!

Advantages

- Helps children and young people to feel that they are viewed as having an important role within the decision-making process of the school.
- It lets the adults know about how they, as children, feel about the decisions made on their behalf.
- It allows the children to take an active role in making the school experience more relevant to their particular needs.
- School Councils develop 'life skills' – the children take ideas and issues forward to a larger forum and learn about reaching a compromise.
- Builds relationships between staff and pupils.

Adaptations

Create a class council with elected representatives to bring forward issues that are more pertinent for the class.

Create sub-groups that have a specific interest in projects, such as making playtime a more enjoyable time for all children.

Have a 'self-elected' council so that more children can be involved in the decision-making process.

Questions for Consideration

How ready are your Senior Managers and Governors to listen and really take on board children's issues and ideas?

Can your Management Team create regular meeting times to include the effective running of a School Council?

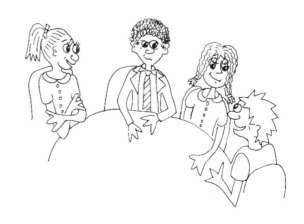

Linked Resources

Peer Mediators – See page 44
Senior Management Team – See page 46

Resource:	'Senior Management Team'

Explanation

An important group of people in your setting is the senior management team (SMT). The team may comprise of the head teacher/manager, deputy head teachers/deputy managers, assistant head teachers, phase leaders, room leaders, advanced skills teachers, Key Stage co-ordinators – there are, in essence, a large number of different people with different managerial roles and responsibilities who may make up the SMT and it is important that you know who these are in your respective setting. Part of their role is to support you in managing the behaviour of the children you work with, be it practically in the setting or through the policies which are developed to drive the practice and philosophy in the setting.

Handy Hints

- Ensure you know who your Behaviour Co-ordinator is so that you can approach them for guidance and support as and when it is necessary. Remember: it is their role to support you and it is not a sign of failure if you seek their advice.
- Encourage members of your SMT to come in and observe you and the children in your learning space/ classroom – this will give them an opportunity to see the kinds of behaviours being exhibited by children in your setting and the ways in which you are trying to manage these.
- Ask to observe members of the SMT with children from their own classes so that they can model good practice for you to take note of; adapt and utilize as part of your own practice.

Advantages

- The SMT is there to guide and support you – it is their job to help you!
- Members of the SMT will have a wealth of experience which they can tap into and share with you.
- Observing the SMT managing undesirable behaviours allows you to see good practice in action.
- Maintaining a healthy dialogue with your SMT is a good way of helping you to keep things in perspective.

Adaptations

Talking to different members of the SMT will yield different responses depending on their age, their experiences and their role.

Work to seek out a range of responses to establish shared and consistent thinking with regard to effective behaviour management strategies.

Questions for Consideration

Do you know all members of your SMT?

When was the last time you spoke to your setting's Behaviour Co-ordinator about the behaviours being exhibited by children in your setting?

When might a member of the SMT be able to come and observe/support you in practice?

Linked Resources

Learning Mentors – See page 42
Midday Supervisors – See page 43

Resource:	'Parents/Carers'

Explanation

Parents/carers are vital resources in managing the behaviour of the children in your setting. Parents influence their children and their behaviour at home in the same way that practitioners/teachers do in your setting. Keeping parents involved in their child's behaviour management ensures that there is a level of consistency between the setting and home – this makes managing behaviour in both places easier and is less confusing for the child.

Parents/carers can be routinely involved in their children's behaviour in the setting using the following approaches: parents' evenings, reports, behaviour diaries, multi-element plans, letters home, phone calls, chatting before and after school, text messages, and messages sent home via the children.

Handy Hints

- Involve parents/carers as much as possible in the management of their child's behaviour.
- Make sure you present yourself as approachable so that parents feel comfortable to talk to you about their child's behaviour.
- Keep parents/carers informed of any issues in class.
- Make sure you send positive messages about children's behaviour home as well as reporting problems – if the children receive positive feedback at home, it will reinforce their positive behaviour in the setting.
- Ensure parents respond to any messages you send home – in some cases this may take a little time and perseverance but is important as you must be sure the message has been acknowledged.

Advantages

- Communication between parents/carers and practitioners/teachers builds an important relationship.
- Children are aware their parents/carers are involved and are motivated and more likely to behave sensibly.
- Parents/carers can give information about their child that can help you to manage their behaviour more effectively.
- Any issues at home that may affect behaviour are more likely to be shared.

Adaptations

Encourage the children to take a role in involving their parents/carers in the management of their behaviour.

Invite parents to help in the setting – the children will respond positively to having their parents/carers with them and as long as ground rules are established, this relationship can be used to support behaviour in your setting.

If you are targeting the behaviour of a particular child, you may ask them to rate their behaviour and to send this information home to discuss with their parents/carers.

Questions for Consideration

Which strategies would you recommend parents to use from other chapters in this book?

How would you approach a parent who does not believe their child is capable of poor behaviour?

Linked Resources

Behaviour Diaries – See page 54
Multi-element Plans – See page 59

Resource:	'Educational Psychologists' (Helen Wilson)

Explanation

An educational psychologist is a fully trained professional who is employed by the Local Authority. Educational psychologists are a valuable resource in managing behaviour – they deal with problems that children and young people may encounter that are too problematic for practitioners/teachers and settings to manage on their own. They help tackle problems which may involve learning difficulties and social or emotional problems. Educational psychologists liaise with other professionals from the education, health and social services. Their work can either be directly with a child or indirectly through work with practitioners/teachers, parents and other professionals. They determine and recommend the most appropriate educational provision and support for the child.

Handy Hints

- If you are concerned about a particular child and feel they may require further support, carry out regular and accurate observations to highlight the issues.
- Liaise regularly with all those who have had, and still have contact with the child (parents, past practitioners/teachers or carers) to gain a wider perspective on what issues the child may be dealing with away from the setting that could be affecting their behaviour.
- Note down key triggers to any particular negative behaviours, and any particular strategies that have been used with the child, both successfully and unsuccessfully, as evidence to support your request for external support.

Advantages

- Educational psychologists carry out a wide range of tasks with the aim of enhancing children's learning.
- They support staff in writing reports for the allocation of particular educational equipment or specialist help.
- They plan learning programmes and collaborative work with other professionals alongside the teacher.
- Practitioners/teachers are exposed to new strategies.

Adaptations

Try using a learning mentor to find a different route into promoting open communication about the problems the child may be facing.

Is there a peer support system in place where an older child can act as a 'buddy' or a positive role model for the younger child?

Questions for Consideration

When new behavioural policies are being devised or reviewed, is their expertise drawn upon?

Are you aware of the whole range of support services available to you as staff when dealing with children with learning difficulties?

Are you aware at what point you can request the support of such services?

Linked Resources

Learning Mentors – See page 42
Speech and Language Therapist – See page 49

Resource:	'Speech and Language Therapists'

Explanation

Young children who have difficulties with their speech or their ability to communicate with others are likely to exhibit behavioural difficulties as they become frustrated with their inability to use language effectively or to be understood by others. Speech and Language Therapists (SLTs) are trained to work with parents, carers and other adults to assess if a child has speech and/or language difficulties and the impact that these might have on their life. If appropriate, the therapist will decide how the child can be helped to reach their full communicative potential. By collaborating together with practitioners/teachers and parents and carers, SLTs can develop interventions, programmes of support and strategies to address these difficulties with the sole purpose of helping children to feel confident and capable of using their language and communication skills to their advantage.

Handy Hints

- Make contact with your Local Authority to find out who your local speech and language therapist is.
- Work in partnership with the SLT so that the advice they give you is shared with your colleagues to ensure a consistent 'plan of action' is implemented to support the children in your setting.
- Consider the value of using communication aids – communication charts and books; words and symbols; and microphones (see www.ace-centre.org.uk/) to help children in your setting communicate.
- Strive to ensure that SLTs have designated physical space available to them when they visit your setting to work with children with language difficulties – this will help them to focus their attention on the children they have come to see.

Advantages

- SLTs have specialized knowledge which can support children with speech and language difficulties to communicate more effectively – this can have a positive effect on children's self-esteem and their behaviour.
- SLTs are also able to offer support and advice about children who have difficulties with eating, drinking and/or swallowing – this may help to address behavioural issues in the dinner hall or during snack time.

Ways in which SLTs can support children

- Training and advice for other service providers, e.g. health and social work.
- Devising programmes of work and ways of supporting children in different environments and by different people.
- Offering assessments and provision of communication aids and resources.
- Getting involved with educational and transitional planning for children.
- Direct therapy with child individually or in a group.

Questions for Consideration

Do you know who your local SLT is? Do you have their direct contact details? (Do remember that they are busy people!)

Which of the children in your setting do you feel would benefit from the support of a SLT? How do you know?

Linked Resources

Multi-element Plans – See page 59
Learning Targets – See page 57

Resource:	'Community Police'

Explanation

One of the important things to remember about behaviour management is that you cannot 'go it alone'. There are a number of different people in the community who can support both you and the children you work with in terms of managing undesirable behaviours. If, for example, the children you work with are not demonstrating appropriate behaviours when they cross the road, or there have been incidents of children 'taking things' which do not belong to them, then seeking the support of your local community police officer is a great way of not only introducing a new person into the setting, but also emphasizing the dangers on the roads, reinforcing road safety practices and instilling in the children the importance of being honest.

Handy Hints

- Ensure that the community police officer who visits your setting is able to talk to children 'on their level' – whilst they might be able to communicate their messages to young people and adults, they need to be able to use a different approach to get their messages across to young children.
- Set up role-play and small-world opportunities where children can 'role play' incidences of concern, e.g. crossing a busy road or stealing the queen's jewels. Work with the children to reflect on how different people feel.
- With the community police officer, work on a strategy to address behavioural issues of concern through the use of puppets, masks, songs, drawing, story books, outdoor play, visits, videos, computer games and dance.

Advantages

- Community police officers can really help to get important messages across to children in an effective and powerful way.
- Young children are fascinated by people in uniforms and this helps to promote healthy respect for those who work in the 'services'.
- Using another person to support you helps to 'share out the load' when dealing with troublesome behaviours.
- Working with the police helps to build positive partnerships for the benefit of the local community.

Adaptations

Community police officers may be called into school settings to talk to older children about 'community' behaviours during a Personal, Social and Health Education and Citizenship (PSHE and Citizenship) lesson, a circle time discussion or during an assembly.

For younger children, community police officers may support the children for a couple of sessions throughout the year; for older children, they may regularly visit the school over a half term/term period.

Questions for Consideration

Do you know who your local community police officer is? How might you be able to find out this information?

Which behaviours would you encourage the community police officer to focus on with the children you work with?

Linked Resources

Senior Management Team – See page 46
Parents/Carers – See page 47

5

Communicating Behaviour
Resources

Resource:	'Stickers' (Helen Wilson)

Explanation

Stickers are sticky labels that come in a whole variety of shapes, sizes, colours and themes. Using stickers is an easy and very effective way to encourage positive behaviour in our early years settings/classrooms. They are an instant response to reward and recognize positive behaviour. Stickers can be used to encourage particular positive behaviours in individual children which can have a positive effect on the behaviour of other children as well. The reward of a sticker can also lead to the repetition of the desired behaviour. When used appropriately, stickers can help to build confidence and self-esteem in children.

Handy Hints

- Display the stickers so that there is an audience for the children's achievement. This will allow you to discuss their progress and use it as an incentive if others are displaying some unwanted behaviour.
- Display the stickers in an appropriate place so that children and adults can view their progress. The more they can see it, the better an incentive it will be and the more you are likely to remember to use it too.
- Once the sticker is awarded, *never* take it away if any negative behaviour is demonstrated. Remember that once a reward is given, it should never be taken back!
- Focus on one behaviour at a time so that the child is clear on what positive behaviour change you are encouraging.
- Make sure all adults are clear on what positive behaviour is being targeted!
- Don't overuse them or they will lose their impact.

Advantages

- This is a very easy and immediate reward system.
- If used consistently and carefully, the sticker system can quickly result in positive behaviour changes.
- There are lots of types of stickers to choose from, from cartoon characters to favourite story book characters.
- Stickers are easily transferable to home so parents can be involved too!

Adaptations

Support staff can set up their own sticker reward system so that the children respond positively to their behaviour management.

Use a target number of stickers to aim for a special treat!

Invite the children to give stickers to each other, being on the lookout for good role models.

Create your own stickers on the computer using blank labels.

Questions for Consideration

How would you involve the children in rewarding stickers? What ground rules would you establish?

In order to keep the strategy fresh, you need to keep a range of stickers. Where could you buy them from?

Linked Resources

Positive Praise – See page 12
Stamps – See page 36
Reward Charts – See page 110

Resource:	'SMARTC Target Board'

Explanation

The SMARTC target board is a useful way of giving children clear direction with regard to making improvements to their behaviour. It can be a display board, a small notice board or a whiteboard – on it are displayed a series of cards on which SMARTC targets are written (these are targets which are Specific, Measurable, Achievable, Realistic, Time-related and Challenging) for particular children to work towards with regard to their behaviour, e.g. *Tom's target is to sit smartly on the carpet for at least three minutes each time he is called to the carpet area during indoor time. This target is to be reviewed by the end of the week (20/10/11).* Once the target has been reviewed and achieved, the child receives a sticker and is able to tear up the SMARTC card and recycle it!

Handy Hints

- Review targets set throughout the session/day to see how well individuals are working towards achieving their targets. Move them closer to the 'target' by displaying the targets on an archery-style target board background to visually show how close the children are to achieving their target (i.e. hitting the bull's-eye).
- Encourage the child's peers to monitor how individuals are doing in relation to their targets, e.g. 'Suzie, have you heard Sally using kind words to anyone this morning?' or 'Phillip, did Mark remember to take turns on the trikes when you were outside?'
- Bring all of the children together as part of the process of reviewing and tearing up the targets once they have been achieved – this helps individuals to develop a real sense of achievement and improvement in their behaviour.

Advantages

- SMARTC targets help to give children a clear direction to what they *should* be doing in the setting.
- Children respond well to SMARTC targets because it helps them to focus on how to be well behaved in small, manageable 'chunks'.
- Over time, you will see progress in the children's behaviour.
- SMARTC target boards are considered to be good practice in educational settings today.

Adaptations

Encourage older children to write their own SMARTC targets in relation to their behaviour; have them record their own targets on the cards.

Allow teaching assistants and other support staff to take on the role of creating and managing the setting and reviewing of SMARTC targets in the setting so that they have a productive and effective impact on the behaviour of children that they work with.

Work with parents and carers to set SMARTC targets for their children at home.

Questions for Consideration

Where would you display the SMARTC target board in your setting? Would you display it at a child-friendly height – why/why not?

Do you think parents and carers would be upset to see their child's name on the SMARTC target board for behaviour? How would you help them to understand that this is meant to be a supportive strategy?

Linked Resources

Behaviour Targets – See page 55
Learning Targets – See page 57

Resource:	'Behaviour Diaries'

Explanation

Behaviour diaries are a great way of supporting and managing behaviour by involving parents and senior management or behaviour specialists. The idea is that a simple diary, in which behaviour is recorded, is sent between home and school. The way in which the behaviour is recorded is something that can be modified according to the needs of a specific child and/or the setting the child attends.

Practitioners/teachers will record behaviour over a number of sessions in the diary, which will then be shared with another member of staff before the diary goes home. The child then takes the diary home and shares the entry with their parents who can discuss both good and bad behaviour accordingly.

Handy Hints

- Involve the child in the notes recorded in the diary: 'What do you think I could say about this morning?'
- Give parents and carers the opportunity to decide what will be commented on in the diary.
- Establish with the child who will see their diary before they take it home: a member of the SMT or another practitioner in the setting?
- Re-state the positive behaviours you want to see from the child at the beginning of each day.
- Make sure you always find something positive to put in the diary at the end of each day.
- Establish a simple reward for repeated positive behaviour, e.g. a certificate or stickers.
- Make time for a short discussion about the day and read what you have written in the diary for the child and reflect with the child what he/she would like to achieve the next day.

Advantages

- Parents will have a good level of involvement with the setting and managing their child's behaviour.
- If there are significant behavioural issues, a member of management is more involved and aware of the support in place.
- Praise can be given for 'good days' from several sources.
- Children have a chance to reflect on their behaviour with both parents and practitioners/ teachers.
- You can easily reflect on behaviour over a period of time and may be able to identify triggers.

Adaptations

This strategy can also be used with a whole class – fill in a diary for all the children that can be collected and recognized by a senior member of staff, much in the same way as a personal diary.

The diary could be sent home in the form of an e-mail rather than as a booklet.

A positive behaviour diary can be designed and sent home with a different child each day depending on who has made the best choices.

Questions for Consideration

Is this a manageable strategy for more than one child?

Could you use another staff member in your setting as a mentor to support the child with the behaviour diary?

Linked Resources

Behaviour Targets – See page 55
Parent/Carers – See page 47
Stickers – See page 52

Resource:	'Behaviour Targets'

Explanation

Sometimes children require specific targets to guide them. For individual children, there will be different triggers for undesirable behaviour and so by creating specific targets for each child you can focus on their individual needs. The following are potential poor behaviours and may be areas you want to focus on when setting a child a target: behaviour in your setting, approaches to work/activities, controlling aggression, organizational skills and personal/social skills. If the children are aware of their area of focus, they are more inclined to take responsibility in managing their behaviour and to be more motivated to do so. Children do not like to be 'kept in the dark' and will appreciate you keeping them informed.

Handy Hints

- Make sure the targets are positive, e.g. write them starting with 'I can' – this demonstrates to the child that you believe that they are capable of making the right choices.
- Make sure the child has access to their target and that it is always visible so other adults in the setting can support the child in achieving the target.
- Make stickers with the target on or stick the target onto the child's desk so that they are reminded of their target.
- Report a child's target to their parents/carers so that they can support you by asking their child about the target each day.
- Tick on the target card when the child achieves their target, and when they have received a pre-agreed number of ticks give the child a reward in the form of a letter, certificate or text message to a parent.
- Ask the other children in the setting to be involved in encouraging the children to achieve their targets: 'Mrs Nocita, I saw Peter making the right choice; he was sharing in the role play corner.'

Advantages

- The children have a constant reminder of what is expected of them.
- The target is very personal to the child.
- Parents are involved and can support their child by discussing progress made in class. The child can also take home the target when they have achieved an agreed number of ticks.
- The children see progress themselves by the number of ticks they have on their personal target.
- All adults in the setting are aware of the target and can be involved in managing the child.

Adaptations

For older children, they could assess their own targets at the end of a session or day.

If the children revert to behaviours after a target has been removed, don't be afraid to re-introduce it but the next time, involve the child in re-writing the target so that it does not lose its effect in motivating them.

Involve an older child in managing the child by asking them to mentor them but make sure you are the one who sends feedback to parents on their achievements in relation to their targets.

Questions for Consideration

How would you feed back to parents on how their child is progressing with their targets?

What reward would be the most effective to use in your setting? Flick through the strategies in the book to give you some ideas.

Linked Resources

Learning Targets – See page 57
Behaviour Diaries – See page 54

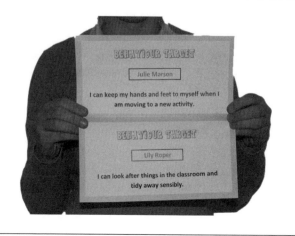

Resource:	'Phone Calls/Text Messages'

Explanation

Many children believe that practitioners/teachers only communicate with the parents and carers of the children they work with through face-to-face means at the start and the end of a session/day. However, we have found a really useful way of promoting positive behaviours in children which has a real effect on the relationships between parents and practitioners/teachers – phone calls and text messages! When a child has been particularly well behaved, practitioners/teachers can make a telephone call or send a text message to the parent or carer; parents and carers usually expect to hear negative things if the setting contacts them so think about how fantastic it is for them to hear something *good* about their child!

Handy Hints

- If the parent or carer is unable to answer the phone, do leave a message on their answerphone as it is a lovely message to pick up later on in the day.
- Make the call yourself as opposed to expecting the setting's/school's secretary/bursar to do it – it has more impact if it is a personal message.
- If you are sending a text message, make sure that it remains professional but positive in tone – avoid 'text-speak'!
- Offer thanks to the parent or carer so that *they* feel they are receiving acknowledgement for their love and support of their child; remember, everyone responds positively to praise!

Advantages

- We have known parents to cry with joy when they hear that their child is behaving well at their setting!
- Children love the idea of their parents and carers knowing that they are well behaved – the more praise and acknowledgement of this, the more children will behave well!
- The child's peers can get involved – we have encouraged the rest of our classes to shout out 'WELL DONE!' at the end of the message we have left for parents/carers at the end of a session.

Adaptations

As opposed to phone calls and text messages, a letter could be sent home to parents and carers about their child's behaviour.

Pictures of the child could be taken with the setting's/school's mobile phone which are then sent to the parent's phone – this could be their new background/screensaver! Do ensure you have the consent of the parents/carers to take images of their children.

Might parents and carers be encouraged to keep you updated with images taken of the behaviours of their children which you are helping them to manage at home?

Questions for Consideration

Do you have access to the most up-to-date contact details of the parents/carers of the children you work with?

Which parents/carers would respond well/not so well to a text message or a phone call about their child? How do you know?

Linked Resources

Behaviour Diaries – See page 54
Letters – See page 58

Resource:	'Learning Targets'

Explanation

Learning Targets are similar to Behaviour Targets but these relate to children's *learning.* They are designed to raise expectations and motivation levels in children by offering them specific goals which they are able to achieve within a designated time frame. Children can be set targets in relation to their counting skills, their understanding of rhyme and rhythm in music, their ability to name different colours, or their willingness to persevere at writing their name – the idea of the target is that it gives the child something to work towards and something which the practitioner/teacher can assess the child by. Children who achieve their targets are likely to receive lots of praise – this boosts their self-esteem and, as a result, they will want more targets to achieve which improves their behaviour as they become more focused on learning as opposed to misbehaving.

Handy Hints

- Set targets which are SMARTC in nature – Specific, Measurable, Achievable, Realistic, Time-related and Challenging.
- Make children aware of what their targets are through verbal and written means; create displays so that parents, carers and other professionals know what children in your class/setting are working towards.
- Regularly monitor how children are progressing towards their targets by observing them as they play/work.
- Establish clear ways in which you will celebrate children's successes and achievements in your class/setting.
- Set targets with actions which can be undertaken in class/the setting and at home so that parents and carers can support their child in the home environment.

Advantages

- Children are less likely to misbehave if they have a clear direction towards achieving something – *simple, eh?!*
- Children who are motivated are less likely to display inappropriate forms of behaviour.
- Children love the praise and attention they get from their practitioners/teachers and their peers when they have achieved their targets.
- Learning targets are a useful contribution to a child's Learning Journey (early years)/assessment portfolio (primary).

Adaptations

For younger children, targets may be set for a couple of hours or for a couple of days.

Encourage parents and carers to support children at home with their targets – consider how they can help their child to meet their targets.

For older children, work with them to develop their own targets so that they have ownership of the direction of their learning – are they self-aware as to their own strengths and limitations?

Questions for Consideration

Where might you display learning targets in your setting?

How long will you make the targets you set last for with the children you work with? Why this long?

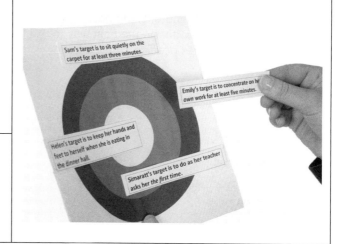

Linked Resources

Behaviour Targets – See page 55
SMARTC Target Board – See page 53

Resource:	'Letters'

Explanation

A lovely way to reward children for their good behaviour is by writing a letter which is posted home to the child's parents/carers. The letter, which should be personalized and not generic in terms of its content, should be written or typed by the practitioner/teacher and offer sincere congratulations to the child for their wonderful behaviour, acknowledging how proud the child's parents/carers are/should be. The letter should offer clear examples as to the kinds of behaviours the child has exhibited and when these have been displayed so that parents and carers have a clear idea as to why the letter has been sent to them. This is a real surprise for parents and carers to open and discuss with their child over breakfast in the morning or over their evening meal together.

Handy Hints

- Ensure that the letter is presented on the setting's/school's headed paper so that it emphasizes the importance of its content.
- Strive to send out letters as soon as possible so that you reward good behaviour *when* it happens; consider using a first-class stamp!
- Avoid sending the letter home with the child – this loses the impact of receiving a letter through the post (no e-mails!).
- Emphasize words if typing the letter (using **bold** or *italics*) to highlight the behaviours you are pleased to acknowledge in their child, e.g. *politeness, kindness, sharing behaviours, turn taking, a positive attitude.*

Advantages

- Parents and carers feel a real sense of pride in their child when they receive a letter about their child through the post – we have known parents to cry at the letter they have received.
- Parents and carers like to keep letters of this nature as evidence of how wonderful their child is – this raises the self-esteem of parents, carers *and* children.
- This is a great point of discussion to have with parents and carers in school/the setting once the letter has been received – this helps to build positive relationships between parents, carers and the setting.

Adaptations

For younger children, focus particularly on behaviours which young children sometimes struggle to show, e.g. *turn taking, putting their hands up to answer questions, sharing, listening to others.*

For older children, focus on behaviours not only in relation to their behaviour but also their learning attitudes, e.g. *perseverance, thinking behaviours, questioning skills, effort levels.*

Questions for Consideration

What if you have parents/carers who have low literacy skills – would a letter be the best way to communicate their child's positive behaviours to them?

How many letters would you send out in a week? Why this amount?

Linked Resources

Certificates – See page 60
Stickers – See page 52

Resource:	'Multi-Element Plans'

Explanation

Multi-element plans are used for a variety of reasons, one of which is to support practitioners/teachers in managing children with behavioural difficulties.

The document should be written with the support of a Special Education Needs Co-ordinator (SENCO) and consists of strategies to follow, as well as SMARTC targets to support and guide the child and practitioner/teacher. The practitioner/teacher reviews the targets regularly, and at the end of each half term/term, the SENCO, parent and practitioner/teacher will meet to discuss the progress the child has made and decide upon the next steps. The practitioner/teacher will sit with the child to compile a list of 'I' statements around a specific behaviour, e.g. if the behaviour was hitting children, the 'I' statements may be as follows: 'I find it difficult to sit on the carpet', 'I want to play.' When the 'I' statements have been collected, these are used to write SMARTC targets for the child in a meeting with the parent/carer and the SENCO.

Handy Hints

- Involve the parents as early as possible; with their support, the targets set could be much more effective.
- Ensure the targets that you make for the children are SMARTC – specific, measurable, achievable, realistic, timed and challenging.
- Make sure there is a reward system in place to encourage the children to stick to their targets.
- Focus on making the targets work for the child and build on skills to help them to manage their own behaviour.
- Put an agreement in place for when things don't go to plan. Make sure there is a strategy for quick intervention and resolution as it is important you help the child to find a way out when things go wrong.
- Use 'I can' at the beginning of each target to motivate the child, e.g. 'I can be kind to my friends'.

Advantages

- You can document the child's progress easily.
- Parents and carers are involved in managing their child's behaviour.
- Collaboration with a SENCO offers an additional perspective on supporting the child.
- If the child requires support from external agencies, there is evidence of steps taken.
- The children are able to share reasons for their behaviour.

Adaptations

If you decide that the child no longer needs a multi-element plan to support them in managing their behaviour. You could design a less formal document for use in your setting.

So that the child can be reminded of their targets, why not give them a copy that they can refer to? Use pictures to support the children if they are unable to read. You could spend a short time each day reminding the children of their targets using their own copy.

Questions for Consideration

Do you think you can write a SMARTC target? Try to write a sample SMARTC target for a child who scribbles on other children's work.

How many targets would you set for a child?

Linked Resources

SMARTC Target Board – See page 53
Parents/Carers – See page 47

Resource:	'Certificates'

Case Study

Every week the children at 'Sunny Smiles Nursery' look forward to finding out who will get a 'Good Choices' certificate. All parents are invited on a Friday when collecting their children to see the certificates being awarded. At the beginning of each week, the children are told what they need to do in that week in order to be awarded a certificate by Ms Stewart. The reasons the certificates are given each week are tailored according to any behaviour that may have caused concern in the nursery over the previous week, for example children sharing, being patient or caring for others. If the children are able to model these behaviours, they are shortlisted for the certificate. The focus for each week is introduced with a story linked to the type of behaviour Ms Stewart is looking for. Every time a child models the focus behaviour for that week, the staff in the nursery ring a bell and praise the child which further reinforces the positive behaviour.

Handy Hints

- Encourage other children to recognize those who are awarded certificates by identifying and mentioning children who are clapping and congratulating those receiving certificates.
- Place a laminated certificate on the wall so that a child who receives an award is recognized throughout the following week.
- Give the children who are awarded certificates expert roles, allow them to be a 'good choices helper' supporting other children in the setting in making good choices.
- Encourage the children to be a part of the presentation – you might even allow the children to present the certificates.
- Certificates can be used in various situations to support behaviour management in your setting – do not be afraid to get creative.
- Use a variety of certificate designs that are relevant to the children.

Advantages

- The children are given something to keep that reminds them of the good choices that they have made.
- Children are able to share their successes with their parents.
- Certificates do not only have to be given to children who produce pleasing work, but they can also be given to children who show sensible/kind/thoughtful behaviour.
- They create an opportunity for collective praise and recognition.

Adaptations

Older children will also appreciate certificates; try to make them more relevant to their age. You could do this by designing certificates signed by famous celebrities. Signatures can be downloaded from the internet.

Allow the children to nominate people who they think deserve the certificate for positive behaviour. Make sure the children do not just vote for friends by asking them to explain why they have nominated someone. This will also help to develop speaking and listening skills.

Questions for Consideration

What would be the best situation for you to award certificates in your setting assembly?

Who would award the certificates?

How often would you award the certificates?

Linked Resources

Individual Reward Schemes – See page 107
Star of the Week – See page 100

Resource:	'Warm Fuzzy'

Explanation

This is an excellent strategy as it involves the children in rewarding each other. A 'Warm Fuzzy' is a little character with wobbly eyes that you can make from anything: pompoms, ping pong balls, tennis balls, elastic band balls and anything else of a practical size.

The children are in charge of this strategy and it is up to you how you work it. You may assign one child to give out a 'Warm Fuzzy' each day for a week or you may ask the child who received the 'Warm Fuzzy' on the previous day to award that day.

A 'Warm Fuzzy' is given to a child that has done something nice for someone else, a child who has been kind and is modelling good behaviour. It's a way to involve the children in recognizing other good behaviour and reinforcing it by giving a small token of appreciation.

Handy Hints

- Ask the children to help you make the 'Warm Fuzzies' as a choosing time activity.
- You may ask the children to decide on a particular behaviour that will be looked for each day by the child awarding the 'Warm Fuzzy'.
- Make sure that the children don't just choose a friend by asking them to share with you beforehand who they have chosen and why.
- You can make the 'Warm Fuzzy' seasonal, giving them a twist depending on the time of year. That way, if the children have more than one fuzzy, they look different!
- Send a note home with a child who receives a 'Warm Fuzzy' so that parents and carers are aware of their good behaviour.

Advantages

- The children have a big part in managing this strategy.
- It is exciting and rewarding, not only for the child receiving the 'Warm Fuzzy', but also for the child awarding it.
- The children can keep a token of recognition for their good behaviour.
- This strategy reinforces positive behaviour.
- The children can be involved in making the fuzzies so they hold more significance when they are awarded.

Adaptations

You could use the strategy with older children but keep it in line with their interests, e.g. you could make simple key rings with celebrities or footballers on them.

Try using a 'Warm Fuzzy' as a playground reward. You can target problem behaviours and reinforce the good behaviour involving midday supervisors and giving them a way to promote good behaviour.

Make larger 'Warm Fuzzies' and award them in assembly as an ultimate recognition!

Questions for Consideration

What behaviours would you target using the 'Warm Fuzzies' in your setting?

Where would you store your 'Warm Fuzzies' in your setting? Would you make a home for them?

Linked Resources

Peer Mediators – See page 44
Midday Supervisors – See page 43
Tremendous Teddy – See page 105

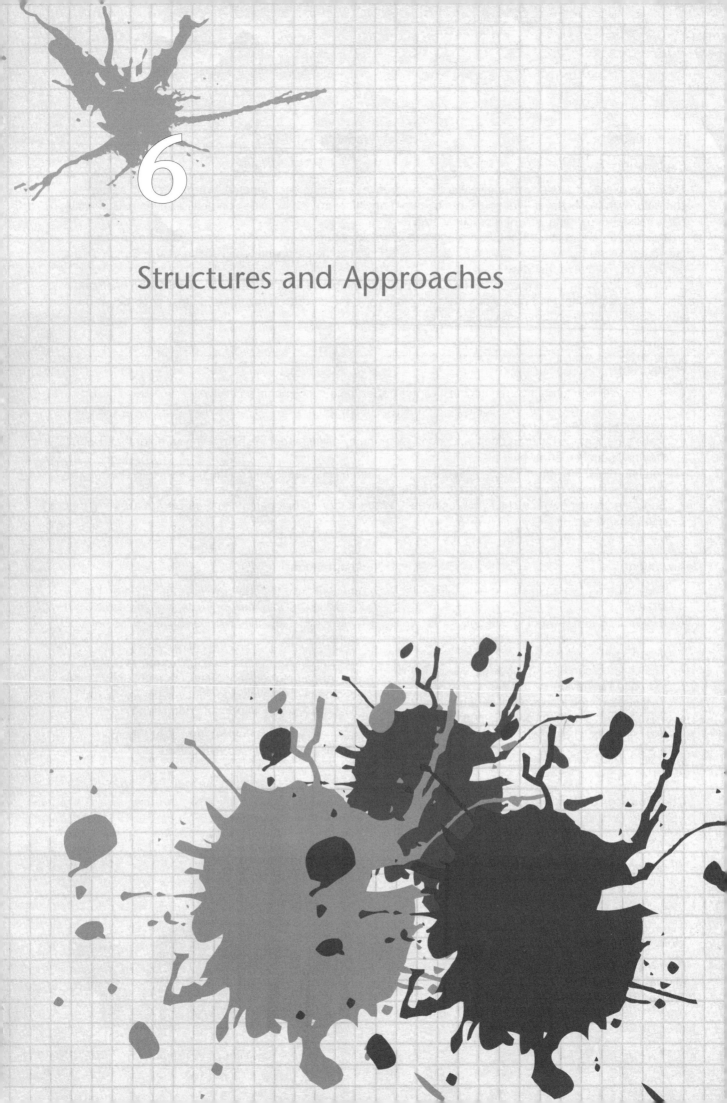

6

Structures and Approaches

Resource:	'Setting Routines'

Explanation

Routines are very important for everyone in an educational setting. They set expectations for the children and the adults and ensure that a setting can run smoothly and efficiently.

Routines can vary in different settings and, depending on the age of the children, may include:

- morning and end of the day routines
- snacks and milk
- special helpers
- register
- hand washing before eating
- getting children's attention
- tidy-up routines
- using the toilet
- moving around the setting.

Handy Hints

- Establish routines early on in the academic year so that children quickly adapt.
- Involve the children in routines, assigning roles and jobs that support the routines in your setting, e.g. you may have children who give out milk and snacks in a nursery setting or children to take the register in a school.
- Encourage the children to decide on what routines are needed, with prompting if necessary.
- Use labels and charts in the setting to support the children in following the routines.
- Make sure your children know why it is important for there to be routines.
- Try not to introduce the children to too many routines at once. Introduce them gradually.
- Set up the role-play corner to encourage the children to practise the routines through play.

Advantages

- Children know what is expected of them from day to day.
- The consistency in the structure of the day can calm some children.
- The more children are a part of the routines, the quicker and more comfortable they become in carrying them out.
- Children with obsessive needs, i.e those on the autistic spectrum, respond well to routine.
- Routines create a smooth transition between activities and sessions.

Adaptations

In a SEN setting, you could concentrate on using visual, auditory and kinaesthetic prompts to support the children in daily routines, e.g. a pictorial timetable and songs to use alongside the daily routines.

Involve older children whenever possible in classroom routines. Allow them to initiate routines and to manage them.

Questions for Consideration

Are there any routines you feel your setting is missing? How could you introduce them?

Are there ways you could observe other practitioners in your setting to see the routines that they use to support you in developing your own?

Linked Resources

Lining-up Award – See page 114
Special Helper Role – See page 17
Special Privileges – See page 111

Resource:	'Outdoor Area' (Helen Wilson)

Explanation

The area and environment that is created outdoors is vitally important in affecting the social development and behaviour of young children. Young children have a great deal of energy and this energy can be channelled into very positive play behaviour if the environment outside is planned for and managed appropriately. Young children should have regular opportunities to play outdoors. Outdoor activities provide stimulation, well-being and happiness, and are the means through which children grow physically, intellectually and emotionally. Outdoor provision is an essential part of the child's daily environment and life. Young children should be outdoors as much as indoors!

Handy Hints

- Let the children plan their own activities outdoors.
- Ensure that all adults understand/are aware of the importance of outdoor areas.
- Make the outdoor area a dynamic, versatile, flexible place where children are in charge of choosing, creating and planning the activities.
- Create a bank of 'irresistible' stimuli to use in the outdoor area, using real experiences and the natural environment, for example water, conkers, leaves, soil, twigs, fir cones and logs.
- Let the children plan activities that involve risk and challenge, but within a framework of safety and security, like building a secret den.
- Access local parks and areas if outdoor space is limited or shared.

Advantages

- The outside environment is free and filled with opportunities for exploration in all areas of learning.
- It allows learning through all of the senses.
- It is an environment in which children can be noisy, active and messy.
- The outdoor environment creates fantastic opportunities for language and literacy, especially with boys.
- Children develop social skills which allow them to manage their behaviour and attitude to others more effectively.

Adaptations

Create areas of 'quiet' and 'secret' for those children who are more reluctant to engage in messy and boisterous play.

Bring in earthy materials, for example logs or chippings to create a more natural environment in restricted space.

Questions for Consideration

Do you and all your staff actively enjoy the outdoor environment?

Are there sufficient and appropriate opportunities and resources to enhance the quality of the outdoor area?

Do you and your staff get actively involved in the children's play outside?

Linked Resources

Teaching Assistants – See page 41
Midday Supervisors – See page 43
Parents/Carers – See page 47

Resource:	'Role Play'

Explanation

Role play is a useful tool to manage behaviour – it can support children in modifying behaviour they have presented from outside of the situation. Children can be encouraged to engage with props and/or interact with a set role-play corner/area. Play allows them to explore scenarios which can be linked to specific behavioural problems in your setting.

A role-play corner should be carefully planned and related to experiences the children are familiar with. The children can then interact effectively and extend their understanding of situations through play and by learning from others.

Participation-in-role play allows children to make decisions about their behaviour away from 'real life' and so they can respond to the reactions of others and modify their behaviour accordingly. The following video can support you in setting up your own role-play corner: www.tes.co.uk/teaching resource/Early-Years-Role-Play-Setting-Up-and-Planning-6038933

Handy Hints

- Incorporate role play into circle time or PHSCE activities as a starter or closer. Put a selection of resources related to your focus on the carpet and encourage the children to interact with a set scenario.
- If a significant behavioural incident occurs, don't be afraid to drop a lesson or activity to work it through using some role play with the children.
- If children are interacting with the role play area through choice, allow them to initiate conversations themselves, but do encourage adults to be involved sometimes as this can enhance discussion.
- While it is important for children to be able to access the role-play area as they choose, you should also be aware that space can become an issue. Have five 'passes' so that only children wearing them can be in the role-play corner, ensuring that the role-play area does not become too crowded.

Advantages

- This strategy encourages play with others and can develop speaking and listening skills.
- It encourages critical thinking through analysis and problem solving.
- Role play allows the children to learn through experience.
- Children can exchange knowledge with their peers.
- It is fun! The children have a great time exploring and imagining.
- Children are naturally drawn to role play.

Adaptations

For older children, you could encourage them to be more independent with the role play. Approach the role play in a structured session as older children are less likely to interact with a role-play corner. Give the children a scenario and a selection of props or clothes associated with a behavioural focus. Ask the children to work collaboratively to prepare a short piece of drama to present to others. Use the performance to initiate a discussion or debate.

Questions for Consideration

What would you put in a role-play area with a focus on caring about others?

How often do you think a role-play area should be updated?

Linked Resources

Knight School – See page 67
Hats – See page 21
Masks – See page 19

Resource:	'Music Sessions' (Helen Wilson)

Explanation

Making music is as much a basic life skill as walking and talking. From a very early age, children learn through the magical process of play that objects and using their body can make an enormous and exciting range of sounds. Music making is a very important behaviour management strategy as certain types of music can calm or stimulate children. The importance of music, rhythm and rhyme is very closely linked to the development of language and pre-literacy skills in young children. A music session in this context refers to children freely exploring music making and selecting music outside a more structured objective-driven music lesson.

Handy Hints

- Collect a range of resources including instruments and 'beaters' and include regular opportunities for children to make and explore sounds and make music both indoors and outdoors.
- Have a wide selection of musical CDs and CD players with headphones for children to have opportunities to explore a range of musical styles.
- Use popular song books mixed with story books in activities so that the children are exposed to the different symbols in music and writing.
- Play music at particular points in the routine, for example snack time or lunchtime, to create a particular mood.

Advantages

- Music is another area in which children can respond individually and express themselves freely.
- Music promotes creativity.
- Repetition in music and song is key to helping children in the early stages of language development. The range of actions/gestures and other props are excellent for supporting early language acquisition.
- Selecting music for a particular part of the session can be used as a reward for positive behaviour.

Adaptations

Link music to topic areas, for example animals, transport, seasons – this can enhance opportunities for expression in language.

Use different music to act as a stimulus to creative activities, for example drawing to jazz.

Use a particular piece of music to signal a particular activity, for example tidy-up time or snack time.

Questions for Consideration

How often do you use music in an unstructured session?

Do you allow children to be music makers on a regular basis?

Are you aware of how important music can be in a child's development?

Linked Resources

Music – See page 25
Sensory Areas– See page 69
Dance – See page 88

Resource:	'Knight School'

Explanation

A truly innovative and creative approach to helping to manage children's behaviour is the notion of 'Knight School'. The idea of 'Knight School' is a simple one – it aims to teach children to be good citizens before they fall into bad habits by engaging them in activities which help them to learn about morals, chivalry and respect. It is based on medieval principals from the Knights of the Round Table which help children to develop confidence and respect for themselves and others. Through individual and group activities, children work to be tidy, clean, honest, hardworking, a team player and polite. 'Knight School' usually lasts for about eight weeks and takes place outside of the setting; however, a number of practitioners/teachers are adapting the principles and practices of 'Knight School' and are using them in their classrooms/settings to positive effect.

Important Considerations

- Boys particularly respond well to 'Knight School', mainly because of the 'knight in shining armour' which they are to try and emulate when in attendance.
- 'Knight School' is a strategy designed for older children (7 to 8 years +) but the principles and practices can be easily adapted and integrated in the provision offered by practitioners/teachers with children below this age.
- There is nothing wrong in encouraging girls to engage in 'Knight School' – the behaviours being promoted are applicable to both boys and girls.
- Visit www.spilsby.info/police/knightschool.htm to find out more about 'Knight School'.

Advantages

- 'Knight School' helps to promote behaviours which we want to encourage in all children, e.g. respect, obedience, gentleness, chivalry and politeness.
- 'Knight School' helps to make 'history come alive' for young children who have little knowledge or understanding about the past.
- 'Knight School' is a very motivating and interactive way of contextualizing positive behaviours for children as they learn about their importance through practical experience and context.

Adaptations

For girls, 'Knight School' could be changed to 'Knightess School'.

'Knight School' can be used as a 10-minute activity each day or as a lesson each week with the children, depending on their age and abilities.

'Knight School' can be used with one group of children or as a whole-setting approach.

Questions for Consideration

How might the children you work with benefit from aspects of 'Knight School'?

Which behaviours would you promote through 'Knight School'?

Do you think there are any implications on resources for setting up/delivering 'Knight School'?

Linked Resources

Role Play – See page 65
Masks – See page 19

Resource:	'Anger Management'

Case Study

Katie was a child in Year 2 who had a very short temper. One day, another child in her group was adding some illustrations to a piece of work they had worked collaboratively on. Katie told him his work was not good enough and that he needed to rub it out and stop. The other child told her that it was his work as well and he could put things on if he wanted to. Katie pulled the other child away from the work, wagged her finger in his face, shouted at him and shook her fist. Katie's teacher, Miss Filbee, asked Katie to take three deep breaths and to go to her angry drawer in the back of the room. Prior to the event, Katie and her teacher had decided on a plan if she started to lose control; in the drawer there was a pillow, a pot of playdough and wax crayons and paper. When Katie needed to she went to the drawer, she used the pillow to hit and scream into, the playdough to pull and the wax crayon to scribble. This allowed Katie to get angry in a safe place so that when the time came she was able to talk to Miss Filbee about the situation without losing control. She was able to talk to her and work through her behaviour, whilst at the same time Katie learned that she was able to step away from a potentially volatile situation with ease.

Handy Hints

- If you have a child who finds it difficult to manage their behaviour, make sure you decide on a plan of action at a time when the child is calm and logical.
- Different strategies will work for different children. You may find that some children need to be alone to regain their composure, while others may need company.
- It is important that the child has input into what is used to calm them. If they are unable to relate to the activities or strategies, then it is unlikely that they will be effective or that they will be used.
- Make sure that there is a discussion following every use of the angry area – it is important to reflect on the behaviour and establish how to prevent it from happening again.
- Ensure the angry area is welcoming for the child.

Advantages

- A potentially volatile situation can be avoided easily.
- The child feels as though their needs are being acknowledged and that they are being listened to.
- The child is involved in managing their own behaviour.
- This is a strategy that can be easily undertaken by parents/carers. Setting up such an area is cheap and practical and can help parents/carers to manage difficult situations at home.

Adaptations

For older children, it could be effective to give them an escape card so if they feel that they are losing control of their emotions, they can leave the classroom before a situation escalates.

Younger children may not be old enough to identify when they need to leave a situation. For children who get very angry, you may devise a checklist of behaviours you look for before taking a child to a calm-down soft area.

Questions for Consideration

Thinking of a child in your setting, which action would you take to support them in managing their anger?

Where could you set up an area to allow children in your setting to calm down?

Linked Resource

Sensory Areas – See page 69

Resource:	'Sensory Areas'

Explanation

Young children need their senses to be stimulated in order for them to remain engaged and focused on their learning; when this does not happen children are likely to misbehave. Sensory areas are a useful way of not only helping to satisfy children's need for sensory stimuli but also in providing a space where children can relax, take time out, reflect and achieve inner calm. Sensory areas come in many different forms and may contain a wealth of different sensory materials on both a large and small scale. Sensory areas can be used as a teaching resource to support children's sensory development and understanding of texture; they are also used to help children to develop a sense of 'awe and wonder', as well as being a place where children can take control of their emotions and think about the effect their behaviour is having on themselves and others.

Handy Hints

- Sensory areas should be made available for children throughout the day so that they can access them as part of their learning and teaching experiences of the day.
- Sensory materials should have tactile and auditory qualities which vary in weight, texture and temperature.
- Objects/items in these areas should also take into account the senses of smell and taste.
- Encourage children who are frustrated to manipulate sensory materials which are malleable.
- For those children who are upset, offer them resources which provide comfort and a sense of connection.

Advantages

- Sensory areas help to promote a sense of well-being in children.
- Sensory areas support children in developing positive behaviours, e.g. exploration, investigation, social skills and physical manipulative skills.
- Sensory areas are a useful environment in which some children feel comfortable to talk to their practitioners/teachers and peers about behavioural incidents and issues.

Adaptations

Sensory areas come in many different forms, e.g. sensory corners, sensory pools, sensory gardens, sensory sheds and sensory play areas. Consider developing one by taking into consideration the age and needs of the children you work with.

The amount of resources found in a sensory area is dependent on monetary funding and space – consider that a wealth of sensory resources may actually over-stimulate children, thus resulting in undesirable behaviours being exhibited.

Questions for Consideration

Where could you set up a sensory area in your setting?

If space and money are an issue, might you be able to create a sensory display or a table-top activity centre for the children you work with as an alternative?

Linked Resources

Music – See page 25
Pictures and Posters – See page 23

Resource:	'Massage'

Explanation

Massage is being increasingly used in settings as a way of helping to manage children's behaviour. It can be used to reduce children's stress levels, and manage aggressive tendencies and the likelihood of bullying occurring. The idea is that the massage is given to the children *by their peers* as opposed to the practitioner/teacher; the child-to-child massage approach is one which is given to their head, arms, back and hands with their permission. Massage time can be used throughout the day to calm children down, improve their motor skills and develop concentration levels/self-esteem. This is a wonderful strategy which children can take home and use with their parents/carers to build caring and tactile relationships.

Handy Hints

- It's a good idea to discuss using massage with your head teacher or manager before you try this out.
- This is a good strategy to use with children aged 4 years old and beyond.
- Using massage with children can help to alleviate many of the behavioural difficulties which make teaching/working with children in the afternoon more challenging.
- Take a look at these wonderful websites – www.misa.org.uk/ and www.massageinschools.com/ – which offer some brilliant guidance and advice about using massage with children.
- Note: You should only really use this strategy if you have undertaken the proper training to get children to massage each other in the correct way.
- Do not pressure children to take part if they are not comfortable.

Advantages

- Massage has a calming effect on children and their behaviour.
- Massage can help to build relationships between children.
- Using massage can help children to understand the importance of appropriate touch and the respect for others.
- Giving and receiving a massage helps to develop essential turn-taking skills.

Adaptations

Some settings are letting children have access to firm sponge balls which they can use to massage their peers with, as opposed to having direct physical contact with their hands.

Some settings are encouraging older children to rub antiseptic hand gel into each other's hands before lunch to protect them against germs.

Children can use child-friendly massage tools if they do not want to have direct contact with their peers.

Questions for Consideration

Do you think the children you work with would respond positively to massage in the setting? Why/why not?

Does this need to be a whole-setting approach, or is it one which you feel you could use just in your own setting – why?

Linked Resources

Sensory Areas – See page 69
Calming Cushions – See page 98

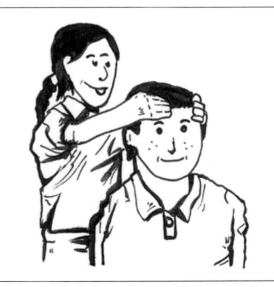

Resource:	'Nurture Groups'

Case Study

Zoe had a very difficult home life. Her parents had recently separated because of her father's violent temper and, as a result, she and her mother had moved into a housing shelter. Zoe was withdrawn and had been displaying some worrying behaviour in the classroom. Her friends had started to play with her less and her teacher was concerned. It was decided, with Zoe's mother's consent, that she would benefit from 'Nurture Group' sessions.

After attending 'Nurture', Zoe began to feel more comfortable and confident with the group leaders and started to speak to them about her experiences, concerns and feelings. The group leaders focused on these experiences and used their knowledge to tackle the behaviours Zoe was presenting in class. After spending time getting to know Zoe, the 'Nurture' leaders supported her as best as they could through this difficult time in her life.

Handy Hints

- Make sure the children have an opportunity to talk during nurture group time if they want. Create a quiet area away from other children.
- Keep the numbers small. If there are too many children, those in the group receive less attention than they may need.
- Do not pressure children to share if they do not want to.
- Keep the nurture session activities calm and meaningful so that the transition back into the setting is easy.
- Offer the children short stories or videos gently linked to experiences the children may have had at home. This can open up the opportunity for discussion.
- Always have more than one adult in a nurture session to ensure children can always talk if they need to.

Advantages

- Children who attend nurture groups are given time and attention that they may not receive at home.
- The children are given space to work through and manage their behaviour in their own time.
- Practitioners/teachers are able to work with the nurture group leaders to support the child.
- Children are taught skills to help them to manage their own behaviour back in their setting.

Adaptations

Allow the children to be involved in what they do in the nurture group sessions. Children who attend nurture groups will often have little say or control over things that are happening at home. Allowing them to be involved in the activities undertaken in the session creates a sense of belonging and control that will make the children feel more comfortable in the sessions.

Refer to www.nurturegroups.org for support in setting up your own nurture group.

Questions for Consideration

How would you decide which children are the highest priority for nurture group sessions?

What would you do to support children in the classroom who would benefit from nurture group sessions but are not high priority?

Linked Resources

Anger Management – See page 68
Sensory Areas – See page 69

Resource:	'Breakfast/After School Clubs' (Helen Wilson)

Explanation

Breakfast and After School Clubs are set up to provide a safe, caring environment offering a range of active, stimulating and restful activities for school-age children before and after school. These care schemes take parental responsibility for the children in their care – as a result, these services must register with the Care Commission and all workers should go through a police check. Services may start between 7.30 and 8.00 am to provide childcare before the start of the school day. This type of service usually consists of a breakfast club which provides children with breakfast. Services will then operate from the end of the school day until 5.30 or 6.00 pm. The majority of clubs are run by voluntary organizations using parent management or advisory groups, but a growing number of clubs are now setting up as community businesses. Out-of-school care clubs are based in a variety of premises including schools, community centres, church halls and nurseries.

Handy Hints

- Get to know the before and after school care organizations and staff who work with your children as you can find out about the activities offered and the behaviours and expectations of behaviour for all ages to try and get a consistent set of behavioural expectations for children.
- Involve and invite staff from these clubs into school to build relationships and to show the children in their care that you are interested in all aspects of their learning and development.
- Get other staff involved in creating consistent policies across all settings.

Advantages

- These clubs offer a range of activities and play equipment all different from, but complementary to, the curriculum.
- They give children the opportunity to socialize and play with other children.
- They support parents and carers, allowing them to take up work, education or training opportunities.
- Parents know that their children will be well cared for.

Adaptations

Set up lunch- and breaktime clubs with children to be run by children with support from staff.

Look into 'after school' activity clubs that concentrate on a particular sport or discipline, for example dance or 'tumble tots'.

Could you find a neighbour or local family who could provide a smaller 'before school service'?

Questions for Consideration

How often do you liaise with the breakfast/after school care staff who look after children that you teach?

Do you involve and invite these staff to events within the school?

Linked Resources

Diet – See page 91
School Council – See page 45
Senior Management Team – See page 46

7

'Timed' Management Strategies

Resource:	'Golden Time'

Explanation

Golden Time is used in many settings as a time children are given, usually on a Friday, which is often used as a method to encourage good behaviour and team work. Practitioners and teachers find that it is a positive strategy to use because children work collaboratively to earn Golden Time and are given a choice as to how the time is spent. It is a very effective management tool as children know that they are in control of how long the Golden Time will be, and what they will do in it. Some settings have a set time period that children earn by collecting points or tokens and others allow children to earn minutes throughout a week varying the length of Golden Time depending on behaviour. The website www.golden-time.co.uk/ can offer you a range of ideas to help you effectively use Golden Time in your setting.

Handy Hints

- Try not to remove Golden Time to sanction negative behaviour; instead, offer it as a reward. If you remove Golden Time as a sanction on a Monday, by the time it reaches Friday the child is still being punished four days later, and they may not even remember why this is.
- It can be effective in building relationships for the children to earn Golden Time for the rest of the class. If a child has been very kind or done some exceptional work, you might announce to the class that this child has earned one minute of Golden Time or a point for the rest of the class.
- The children could earn Golden Time in minutes or you may want to arrange it so that they collect a certain number of points to receive Golden Time.
- Offer the children a selection of choices and decide together what will be done in Golden Time, but do not decide for them.

Advantages

- The children need to work together to receive a reward, so this is a great way to build class relationships and trust.
- Parents and carers could work with their children at home with a similar reward scheme.
- It is exciting for the children and a lovely period of time for you to get to know and interact with them.
- Golden Time is a strategy that can be easily used with children of all age ranges and of different needs.

Adaptations

The children can work either as a class, year group or school to earn Golden Time.

Children in Key Stage 2 also enjoy golden time. Perhaps re-name it to make it feel more 'grown up' for these children and suggest that they can timetable the Golden Time in advance, choosing activities they would like to do.

You may have a special Golden Time for a small number of children who have been particularly well behaved. Do something slightly different to the others, for example a visit to the park, cooking, afternoon tea with the head teacher/setting manager.

Questions for Consideration

Do you think it would be appropriate to take Golden Time minutes away from a child?

What activities would you offer the children in your setting to do during Golden Time? Make a list as a selection for them to choose from.

Linked Resources

Afternoon Tea with the Head Teacher – See page 108
One-to-One Time – See page 77

Resource:	'Circle Time'

Explanation

Circle Time is highly effective in developing a supportive and co-operative classroom. With regular sessions, children learn to show respect for their peers and develop skills to help them work through challenging situations. Circle Time can be instigated following an incident in the classroom or can be planned as part of a series of learning and teaching experiences.

Case Study

Ms Mortimer noticed over a week that there was one child in her class that was being pushed out by the other children. She decided to tackle this problem by using a Circle Time session to encourage the children to empathize with others. Ms Mortimer changed her timetable that day and carried out a Circle Time session with a focus on bullying. The next day, when it was obvious that this particular child was being excluded, Ms Mortimer asked questions about the session on the previous day. This discussion put the issue into context for the children and allowed them to realize the way they would feel in this situation which prompted them to include the child who was being left out.

Handy Hints

- Play games that encourage teamwork – team games develop the children's ability to work collaboratively in other activities and collaborative work promotes an awareness of others.
- Prepare a folder that you can add ideas and games to as you teach Circle Time; split these ideas into focus areas and you will have a bank of resources you can dip into.
- Use an object that the children can hold, showing that it is their turn to speak.
- Allow the children to share their ideas but remember that it is difficult for young children to listen attentively for long periods of time.
- The Circle Time website (www.circle-time.co.uk) offers a range of strategies to support you in leading effective Circle Time sessions.

Advantages

- This strategy is an excellent tool for encouraging respect for others and building a form of preventative behaviour management.
- Circle Time can be a lot of fun for the children as they can learn through games and interactive activities.
- It is a great time for you to get to know the children and their ideas and opinions.
- Circle Time encourages turn taking and listening to others.

Adaptations

Children in PVI settings may benefit from smaller groups in Circle Time. By limiting numbers, the children will have less time to wait in the games and more focus can be put on responses given by others.

Older children may find Circle Time a little tedious. Allow the children to lead the sessions and decide on what will be focused on. Giving the children ownership makes the sessions more relevant to them and their personal experiences.

Questions for Consideration

If you are struggling for space in your room, where in your setting could you take the children to do Circle Time?

How might you approach a sensitive issue, such as bereavement, in your setting, using Circle Time?

Linked Resources

Bubble Time – See page 76
Knight School – See page 67

Resource:	'Bubble Time'

Explanation

Bubble Time (or 'chat time' as we like to call it) is a device devised by Jenny Mosley which allows children to ask for one-to-one time to talk with an adult. Every child in the setting has their name printed on a 'bubble' (a circular piece of card) which has a peg attached to the back of it. If the child wants to talk to the practitioner/teacher, they can take their name 'bubble' and attach it on to the outside edge of a large class 'bubble' on the wall which indicates to the practitioner/teacher that there is someone who wants to talk to them. During the session/lesson, when it is appropriate, the practitioner/teacher will take the child's name 'bubble' off the large bubble and will then have some one-to-one time with the child, addressing and supporting the child with any personal issues they have, such as the behaviour of others.

Handy Hints

- Talk to the children in your setting about how the large bubble works, e.g. if the children imagine that the large bubble is a clock and a child puts their name 'bubble' where the number one would be located, this means that the practitioner/teacher will speak with that child *first*. If another child puts their name 'bubble' on the large bubble they have to put it *next to* the first name bubble which means the practitioner/teacher will speak to them *second*.
- Ensure the children understand that Bubble Time is about helping to deal with children's personal issues which might link to the behaviours of others, e.g. if they are being bullied at school or they have been hurt in the playground by aggressive peers; issues with their learning can and should be addressed during class time.

Advantages

- Bubble Time helps children to 'release' their thoughts and feelings through words in a safe place and at an appropriate time; this helps to reduce behavioural difficulties in class.
- Children quickly learn what they should use Bubble Time for in terms of the things they should bring to the discussion with the practitioner/teacher.
- Practitioners and teachers are very busy people and sometimes it is difficult to find time to really listen to children – Bubble Time facilitates this.

Adaptations

Bubble Time for younger children can be used to talk about things the child wants to talk about, e.g. what they had for lunch or who their friends are. If young children are not allowed to talk, they can become very frustrated which can lead to behavioural difficulties.

Bubble Time for older children can be used both in the classroom and in the playground if midday supervisors wish to use it during lunchtime.

Questions for Consideration

If you work in a large nursery, do you think Bubble Time would be useful with your children? Why/not?

If you do not already use Bubble Time with your children, how do you ensure that you have time to have a one-to-one with your children?

Linked Resources

Circle Time – See page 75
One-to-One Time – See page 77

Resource:	'One-to-One Time'

Case Study

Gemma came from a very large family and had a troubled home life. She found it difficult to socialize with other children and struggled to make friends. Gemma had a tendency to take things from others and to hurt children on the playground. In order to encourage her to make good choices, the practitioners in her setting decided that they would reward her when she was able to complete a session with no behavioural issues with 10 minutes of one-to-one time with an adult of her choice. Because her family was so large, it was rare that Gemma had the full focus of an adult and this time allowed her to be the centre of attention without having to resort to poor behaviour. This strategy proved so successful that eventually Gemma was asked to invite a friend to join in the sessions. The practitioners in the Foundation Unit used this as an opportunity to support her in working on her social skills and building relationships.

Handy Hints

- Children do not have to misbehave to be offered one-to-one time as a reward; the strategy could also be used to promote positive behaviour in children who usually make good choices.
- Ask the children to decide what they would like to do in the one-to-one time so that they enjoy and look forward to it.
- If children are struggling to decide what they would like to do in the one-to-one time, offer a selection of options. Here are some ideas: card games, tricks, reading a book, playing a board game, drawing a picture, or even just talking!
- Ensure you have the one-to-one time in a quiet space away from other children so that it is private and you are undisturbed.
- It may be that the child would like to do the one-to-one time with a different adult for some sessions – accommodate this wherever possible.

Advantages

- This strategy is very effective because the children recognize how special it is to have your time.
- Parents can easily adapt this strategy for use at home; it could even be used to offer an activity away from home, spending time with one or both parents on their own.
- It is relatively easy to organize and an excellent incentive for the children.
- If you allow children to invite a friend, they are able to share their successes.

Adaptations

Older children may not want to spend time with their teacher; you could offer the children time with older pupils. Perhaps invite those who are in the year above to spend time with them. Allow the children to be involved in who they would like to have their special time with but remember to speak to the older pupils' teachers.

Invite the children to choose who they would like to work with.

Questions for Consideration

How would you ensure this strategy stays fresh and continues to have an impact in your setting?

What would you do if you were absent and had arranged one-to-one time with a child?

Linked Resources

Peer Mediators – See page 44
Bubble Time – See page 76

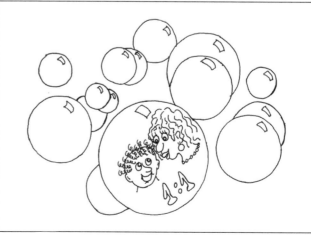

Resource:	'Assemblies'

Explanation

For those children in maintained schools, it is a legal requirement for pupils to attend a daily assembly. Assemblies are a time during the day when children and practitioners/teachers come together for a short time for collective worship to be delivered. Assemblies can be a very useful way of helping to address behavioural difficulties, not only with the children in your class but also across the entire school. Practitioners/teachers can do this by using stories, largely from the Christian faith but also the other five world faiths, to teach the children about honesty, politeness, love, honour and respect for others. There are times when the focus of these assemblies may be more appropriate for a particular Key Stage; this means that assemblies can be differentiated to ensure that the messages presented to children are age-appropriate and meaningful.

Handy Hints

- Use assemblies to respond to issues or deal with events that occur from time to time in the school setting, e.g. issues of conflict, racism, bullying, and making new children feel welcome in the school.
- Plan assemblies to last for 10–15 minutes maximum for Key Stage 1 children – the longer the assembly, the less likely the 'message' will stay with the children as they will become restless and inattentive.
- Use props, music, dance, role play, questions and answers, songs, video footage, stories, pictures, ICT applications, humour and costumes to engage and maintain the attention of children during assembly time.

Advantages

- Assemblies are a useful way of getting a consistent message across to a large number of children in a relatively short period of time.
- Children enjoy and learn from assemblies when they are made interesting and interactive and the 'message' of the assembly is clear to them.
- Assemblies help practitioners/teachers to address issues in a way which does not 'name and shame' individuals but promotes a whole-school approach to the addressing of behaviour difficulties.

Adaptations

For young children (0–3) assemblies are not appropriate. Use activities throughout the setting or story time to address behavioural issues.

A number of settings encourage Foundation 2 (reception/kindergarten) children to attend the school's assembly time. Build this up slowly over the year so that the children have experience of attending this once a week; by the end of the summer term they should be ready to attend every day when they move into Year 1.

Encourage parents and carers to attend assemblies so that they are aware of the behavioural difficulties and how these are being addressed in your school.

Questions for Consideration

How often do you use assemblies to respond to behavioural difficulties in your school?

Do you use visitors to support delivery of the assemblies in your school? If so, what input do you offer them in terms of making them aware of the current 'behavioural climate' in your school?

Linked Resources

Community Police – See page 50
Senior Management Team – See page 46

Resource:	'Lunchtime'

Explanation

Every practitioner/teacher knows that lunchtime is a particular period of the day when children's behaviour can become a little challenging! Sometimes children forget how to behave when they are in the dinner hall and on the playground, and this can cause issues for the midday supervisors, the kitchen staff, other children in the school and the practitioners/teachers who have to deal with these issues when lunchtime is over. There are a number of simple strategies which you can use to overcome the common issues of noise, rudeness, silliness, fighting and general inappropriate forms of behaviour during this period of the day; these are offered in the 'Handy Hints' section below for you to select from and use.

Handy Hints

- Remind children of the behaviours you expect them to model during playtime; might the children themselves be able to tell you of the behaviours you expect of them?
- Play quiet, calming music in the dinner hall – if the midday supervisors cannot hear the music then the children must be too loud.
- Occasionally sit with your children in the dinner hall so that you can model appropriate ways to sit, eat and talk.
- Encourage midday supervisors to award stickers and stamps to children who behave well during lunchtime.
- Work with the senior management team to monitor behaviours of the children in the setting during lunchtime – are there particular classes or groups of children who need to be targeted with particular strategies?

Advantages

- A little time invested by yourself during lunchtime can have a really positive effect on the behaviours of the children you work with, and of others in the setting.
- Midday supervisors are particularly grateful for any support you can give them in relation to managing the behaviour of children in the setting; remember that they are not trained practitioners like yourself.
- Children will enjoy lunchtime more if they know how they should behave during this time.

Adaptations

Encourage older children to act as 'Behaviour Monitors' during lunchtime, spotting children who are being well behaved and identifying those who are exhibiting undesirable behaviours.

Occasionally encourage support staff to sit with children during lunchtime so that they are able to contribute to the positive lunchtime behaviours of the children you work with.

Use PSED/circle time/PHSCE opportunities to talk about good lunchtime behaviours with the whole group/class.

Questions for Consideration

How often do you sit with your children when they go into the dinner hall? What effect do you think this might have on their behaviour if they know you are going to be sitting with them?

Which specific lunchtime behaviours do you think you need to 'target' with your children to address key issues during lunchtime?

Linked Resources

Midday Supervisors – See page 43
Circle Time – See page 75

Resource:	'Brain Breaks'

Explanation

Brain Breaks are simple little activities which last for less than a minute and are designed to give young children's brains a little rest throughout the session/lesson. Concentrating for long periods of time can be tiring for some children; Brain Breaks give children a little respite from their learning, helping them to stay focused, concentrate and re-energize themselves when they return to their activities. From stretching and shaking parts of the body to purposefully yawning, Brain Breaks can give both you and the children a 'breather' from the stresses and strains of learning and teaching so that children's behaviour does not become unsettled or disruptive as they progress through a session/lesson/day.

Handy Hints

- Prepare a laminated card which offers details of lots of different Brain Break activities which you can select from throughout the session/lesson.
- Consider using some of the Brain Break ideas on www.behaviourmatters.com/articles/Brainbreaks.pdf and www.teachingexpertise.com/articles/raising-achievement-using-brain-breaks-645.
- As the children become familiar with these little activities, encourage individuals to lead the delivery of the Brain Break activities.
- Some children may consider these activities as a little 'silly' so it is important for them to understand their importance in relation to their learning through your explanations and modelling of the activities.

Advantages

- Brain Breaks can improve learning, teaching and behaviour in the setting.
- Children love Brain Breaks as it helps to break their learning into manageable chunks.
- Kinaesthetic learners in your group/class (those who learn through movement) respond extremely well to Brain Break activities.

Adaptations

Brain Break activities can be adapted in many ways, depending on what the practitioner/teacher and the children would like to do and perform; be creative by adding sound effects, routines and game play to your Brain Break repertoire!

For older children, use Brain Breaks every 25–30 minutes to support children in hour-long lessons/sessions.

Questions for Consideration

Which ideas would you use with the children you work with?

During which activities/periods of the day would Brain Breaks be particularly useful? Why so?

Linked Resources

Activate to Concentrate – See page 90
Physical Games – See page 89

Resource:	'End of Term/Year Awards Assembly' (Helen Wilson)

Explanation

The end of term or year awards assembly is an opportunity for the whole setting to come together and celebrate the achievements of children across the whole age range. Children from each year group or class are chosen by their teachers for specific awards, for example attendance, concentration, sporting achievements – whatever you like! They are recognized in front of their peers and either get to keep the award or keep it for the term or year before handing it on to the next recipient.

Handy Hints

- Do not have too many awards/trophies as the process becomes very long and tiresome for those who have not won an award.
- Make sure the awards presented are valued by the children!
- Always check to see who has won an award previously. Don't always award the same children, as it can be very de-motivating.
- Include an award that is worked for over a period of time and linked to a particular desired behaviour that has been sustained over that period.
- Laminated certificates are cheap but long-lasting reminders of the award received.
- Get last term's/year's recipient to present the award!

Advantages

- This is a very simple but public celebration of children's achievements.
- Younger children are inspired by the older children.
- If you are re-using trophies, it is a very inexpensive event.
- It is a great way of reinforcing desired behaviour throughout the setting.

Adaptations

Get the children to create an award that is personal to their class.

Get the children to vote for the winner and add the votes to the staff vote; this will make the whole process more exciting!

Create an 'X' factor award that recognizes something individual and special in a child.

Have a class award ceremony with awards that are relevant to particular behavioural targets of the class.

Questions for Consideration

How do you recognize and reward the child who is quietly consistent in all aspects of school life?

When did you last review the awards? Are they still relevant and meaningful to the children?

Who *decides* on who receives the award and who is the best person to give the award?

Linked Resources

Certificates – See page 60
Reward Charts – See page 110
House Points/Table Points – See page 112

Resource:	'Detention'

Explanation

Detention is defined by the Oxford Dictionary as 'the punishment of being kept in school after hours' and is often associated with secondary education. In early years settings, detentions can be used but in an age-appropriate way. They should be presented as a form of 'Time Out' for children.

Examples of detention in early years settings can include missing playtime, outdoor play, golden time, choosing time, cookery or any other recreational activities that the children enjoy.

It is important that if a child is given detention that the sanction is given that day and is not carried over to another. It is likely that with young children they will not remember the reasons for the detention if it is carried over, and the detention will simply leave the child feeling sad and wondering why they can't join in with other children.

Handy Hints

- Do not announce the detention to the rest of the class – the child has already had their punishment, so avoid adding to it!
- If children are missing parts of playtime or golden time, allow them to watch the other children enjoying themselves to remind them that a choice they have made has resulted in them missing a fun activity.
- Make sure the amount of time a child is put into 'detention' is realistic according to their age.
- Before allowing the children to re-join others, discuss the reasons why time out was given – reflecting on their behaviour reinforces their understanding of why the behaviour should not be repeated.
- Refer the detention to the choices the child made. Make sure the child understands that they are there because of a decision that they made. Help the child to understand that they have control of their own choices – they decide if they are rewarded or if they receive a sanction.

Advantages

- It is a tried and tested form of behaviour management that can be easily modified for all ages.
- The children are made aware that they are in control of the decisions that they make and the consequences those decisions have.
- In early years settings, children are able to see what they are missing and will try not to repeat the same mistakes.

Adaptations

Key Stage 2 children are generally familiar with detention. For older primary children, the same strategies can be used but with modified timings. Detention in primary-aged children should not extend outside school hours.

For children with SEN, consider the time frame of the sanction. It is important that they are able to recognize that the punishment is a consequence of their behaviour and that the two are linked.

Questions for Consideration

What would a detention be used for in your setting?

How could you ensure the children are not 'forgotten' about when carrying out their detention?

Linked Resource

Thinking Chair – See page 97

Resource:	'Stop–Think Lollipop'

Explanation

The 'Stop–Think lollipop' is a circular piece of card fastened to a round piece of dowel. On one side of the card is a STOP road sign; on the other is a picture of a light bulb (this represents the 'Think' part of the 'Stop–Think lollipop'). The lollipop is an effective way of managing inappropriate behaviour without the teacher/practitioner having to use their voice. If a child is seen to be behaving inappropriately, the practitioner/teacher simply needs to hold the lollipop up to them so that the child 'Stops' what they are doing. When this happens, the practitioner/teacher simply turns the lollipop around to show the light bulb which encourages the child to think about their behaviour and to decide what they can do to improve it.

Handy Hints

- Talk to the children in your setting about how the lollipop works; in essence it strives to promote self-evaluation and reflection as the resource uses images to direct the children, e.g. Stop and then Think about their own behaviour and what they could do to rectify it.
- Have smaller versions of the Stop–Think lollipop so that other adults can use these with small groups of children.
- Use the lollipop to manage behaviours which are persistent with children, e.g. calling out, talking over the teacher/lead practitioner, and being 'off task'.
- Ensure that the colours and images used on the lollipop are bright and clear so that children can clearly recognize them.

Advantages

- The lollipop is a quick and easy resource to make and use with children.
- Children will quickly respond to the Stop sign as it has direct links with road signs in the environment.
- The lollipop encourages children to think about their own behaviour in terms of what they are doing which is deemed to be inappropriate and gives them the chance to amend their behaviour for the better; this saves the practitioner/teacher having to always 'direct' the child.

Adaptations

For younger children, the lollipop could just have a Stop sign as it is difficult for them at that age to self-regulate their own behaviour due to developmental stages.

For older children, the practitioner/teacher could ask the child to verbalize what they might do to change their behaviour so that the practitioner/teacher has an idea of what the child is thinking.

Questions for Consideration

Do you think that the Stop–Think lollipop would work well when the children are in the outdoor play area/playground? Why? Why not?

Would you use this resource with children who have special educational needs? Why? Why not?

Linked Resources

Referee Cards – See page 33
Stop and Go Cards – See page 35

8

Influential Management Strategies

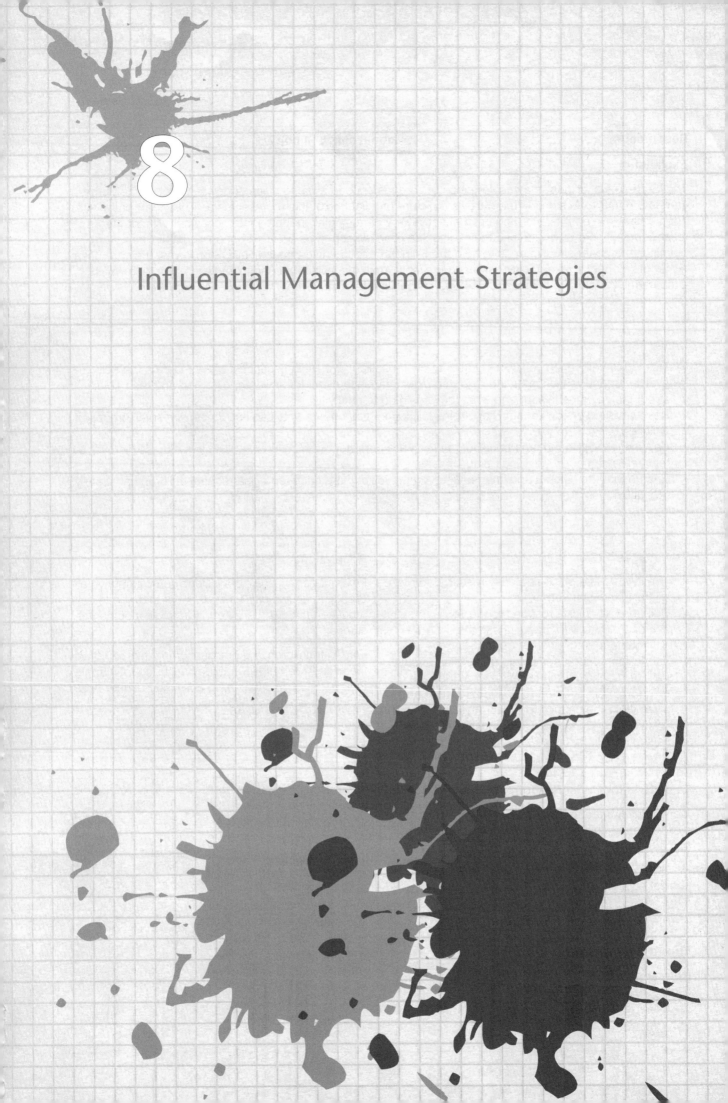

Resource:	'Layout of the Setting'

Explanation

Your setting should promote well-being for all the children in your care. The layout of your setting can have a profound impact on the behaviour of children. If the children are working in a setting that suggests to them that they have been considered in the way it looks, they are more likely to focus, be motivated and, as a result, learn more from experiences/lessons. It is important to think about the way the furniture is structured and what size it is; do the children have room to work without bumping into each other? It is also important that displays are on the correct level; children should be able to interact with the displays and cannot do this if they are out of reach. Maslow's Hierarchy of Needs should help you to consider the classroom layout in your setting; often children will not have these needs met at home and so by demonstrating to the children that you are considering their needs, they are more likely to feel cared for and more likely to behave.

Handy Hints

- Consider what you value in your own space and try to include elements of this in your setting.
- If a setting is too busy, it can be over-stimulating for the children which confuses them and can lead to poor behaviour as the children struggle to concentrate on what they are doing.
- Ensure the teaching space is engaging but not cluttered – the children should not feel squashed!
- Make sure the children have their own personal space in the setting: a drawer, a peg, a 'cubby hole' to put their belongings in which will give the children a sense of belonging.
- Ensure the children recognize that they can access things freely, as they may not be sure what they are allowed to touch.

Advantages

- By focusing on the needs of the children, they will be happier in the setting and are more likely to achieve.
- If you concentrate on the individuals in your care and plan the layout of your setting accordingly, the children will be calmer and the setting will run more smoothly.
- By focusing on making things more accessible for the children, you are encouraging independence.
- If the children are happy, the practitioners/ teachers will also be happy.

Adaptations

For children with specific needs, the layout of a setting can hold particular importance, especially for those on the autistic spectrum. Consider the individual needs of these children when planning the layout of the setting.

If you work in an open-plan setting, organizing the layout needs to be done as a team. It will be far more effective to have input from everyone, and all practitioners will find it easier to support children in the setting if they have had an input into the layout.

Questions for Consideration

Think about your setting – how do you feel about the layout after reading about this strategy? Is there anything that you would like to change?

Can you attribute any behaviours (positive or negative) of the children in your setting to the layout?

Linked Resources

Setting Routines – See page 63
Displays – See page 16

Resource:	'Learning Styles'

Case Study

Teaching in a particularly difficult class, Mr James found engaging all children in group work challenging. The children were disturbing and distracting each other while he was trying to teach. He decided that a way to improve the children's behaviour could be a consistent multi-sensory approach to learning. During carpet work the children were exposed to visual and auditory prompts through the use of an interactive whiteboard and Mr James' voice. Wherever possible, for the kinaesthetic learners he used interactive activities on the whiteboard or gave the children mini whiteboards to record thoughts, pictures or responses – this meant that all learning styles were catered for. After implementing the multi-sensory approach to teaching, Mr James found that the length of time the children remained focused improved greatly. The next step, to assure the engagement of all children and to reduce behavioural incidents for Mr James, is to refer to learning styles in his planning to ensure that children are catered for in lesson time as well as in whole-class work.

Handy Hints

- Present activities with a selection of options focusing on specific learning styles and allow the children to make a choice about how they would like to complete the activity.
- Use a variety of media to ensure all learning styles are catered for.
- Make the children aware of their learning styles so that they can support their learning and access resources suitable to their learning style.
- Read about Howard Gardner's Multiple Intelligences Theory which offers a more detailed approach to supporting preferred styles of learning and can be used to support planning and teaching in early years settings.

Advantages

- Children are engaged and so good behaviour occurs naturally. Often, but not always, children behave badly to curb boredom.
- The children are not only likely to behave more sensibly, they will also learn more.
- Considering and planning with a focus on learning styles makes for a better lesson.
- As a teacher/practitioner, you are responding to the needs of the children in your setting.
- After a short time focusing on this strategy, it will come naturally when planning to consider learning styles.

Adaptations

Involving older children in managing their learning style can have a positive effect on their general behaviour and attitude to work.

Ask older children to identify ways in which an activity can be made accessible for all learning styles.

Move on to using Gardner's Multiple Intelligences to refine the activities for the children.

Questions for Consideration

How could you establish the learning styles of the children in your setting?

Would you modify assessments on the children depending on their learning style?

Linked Resources

Activate to Concentrate – See page 90
Instructions – See page 94

Resource:	'Art and Design'

Explanation

Art therapy is often used to support children to manage behavioural problems and to encourage children to express their emotions in a safe environment.

Art therapy can be a very effective preventative form of behaviour management. It is a strategy that is put in place to try to facilitate positive change by allowing the children to be physically involved with materials, making a significant object, and also through the interaction of the person working with them.

By working with children in either a one-to-one or small group setting, children are working in a safe environment and are more likely to feel comfortable and to respond positively to the relationship that they build with the person leading their therapy group. As the children become more comfortable and willing to express themselves, they may be able to work through and manage their behaviour themselves when in their setting, using strategies they have previously learned in art therapy.

Handy Hints

- Encourage the children to attend regular therapy sessions outside of taught sessions/lessons so that they can receive continued reliable support.
- This strategy can also be used in a moment of crisis in your setting to support children who are finding it difficult to express their emotions.
- Use a variety of artistic approaches to cater for different children and maintain the effectiveness of the strategy.
- Research art therapy websites to give you ideas for activities that you can use with children in your setting.
- Encourage the children to be involved in the work done in sessions to keep the activities relevant for them.
- Try not to have rigid session outcomes as the work the children produce should be their own – it is important you do not tell the children how to express themselves.

Advantages

- Art therapy allows for children who have existing behavioural problems to be supported in a safe environment.
- The children are offered a multi-sensory way to express themselves, which can also expose them to strategies that can help them to self-manage their behaviour.
- The therapy is an effective method to use for children of all ages as well as with children with SEN.
- The sessions can allow most children to recognize, and with time, control the emotions they are feeling.

Ideas for Sessions

- Finger painting to music – the children's senses will be stimulated to support them in producing creative work.
- Outdoor art – encourage the children to draw the patterns or shapes that they see in the clouds or flowers/plants.
- Group collage – encourage the group to create their own collage and then put the work together to create a patchwork.
- Emotion paintings – talk about feelings and choose colours associated with those feelings. Encourage the children to use strokes that relate to these emotions. See:

1. http://teach-nology.com/teachers/lesson_plans/special_ed
2. www.arttherapyblog.com/child-art-therapy/art-therapy-changes-lives-of-abused-children

Questions for Consideration

What would you need to start an art therapy group in your setting?

Who would benefit from art therapy in your setting?

Linked Resources

Dance – See page 88
Physical Games – See page 89

Resource:	'Dance'

Explanation

Dance is an excellent tool to use with children to support behaviour management because it is a great way to express feelings and emotions. There are many dance styles and they all focus on expressing a certain emotion/attitude, e.g. tango = passion; hip hop = enjoyment/relaxation; Irish = control/grace. Dance can help children to understand how to express themselves. If children can relate to and express an emotion/attitude associated with dance then they are more likely to be able to understand their own emotions. Hopefully, in time, this will support them in managing and controlling these emotions in everyday situations. The music the children dance to can also have a positive impact on their behaviour and the way that they respond to dance, especially if you use music the children can relate to. Dance can be used to teach children the skills to calm and relax themselves that they can apply during times of need. It can also be used as an immediate outlet for anger or frustration.

Handy Hints

- Use dance as part of Brain Gym or to calm the children following an exciting playtime (choose your dance style wisely!).
- Involve the children in dance, allowing them to be a part of both music selection and choreography.
- Use different dance styles to see which works the best with your children. Which style do they prefer? Which music or dance style is the most effective for certain children?
- Don't create a complicated piece of dance; the dance is not for the West End stage. Keep it simple and the children are more likely to remember the steps and routines and enjoy themselves.
- Encourage the children to respect others; the children need to be comfortable and not self-conscious for this strategy to be effective.

Advantages

- This is a physical form of behaviour management, which is memorable and will support kinaesthetic learners.
- It is fun for you and the children, and can be easily resourced.
- The children are keeping fit while learning to express and manage their emotions and feelings.
- Children can be exposed to dance from different countries and cultures, encouraging international mindedness.

Adaptations

You may find that the ways in which you use dance will need to be adapted according to the needs of the children. Younger children can still be exposed to a variety of dance styles and music but they will need to be shown very basic and repetitive steps.

Encourage older children to support younger children in this strategy. Invite them to come and model/teach new dance styles to the children.

Questions for Consideration

How would you make sure that there is room for this strategy in your setting?

How will you improve your knowledge of dance to be able to use this strategy effectively?

Linked Resources

Music – See page 25
Physical Games – See page 89

Resource:	'Physical Games' (Helen Wilson)

Explanation

Physical games are a really useful, fun, free and very effective way of promoting and managing aspects of behaviour with young children. They allow an opportunity to 'let off steam' in a safe environment and they can also be used to promote desirable positive behaviour – for example, there is a whole wealth of games that focus on children using co-operative skills through physical games. More importantly, the regular inclusion of physical games improves the health and well-being of children and can reduce the risk of developing many chronic illnesses in later life. In the short term, they can also help aid concentration!

Handy Hints

- Make warm-ups an integral part of every session – do some stretching/moving before starting an activity.
- Before you start, get everybody's attention so that you can explain the rules of the activity. Always make sure to say the 'when' before the 'what' of the game, for example 'When I say "Now" I want you to find a partner'.
- Make sure everybody is involved and engaged. Don't choose formal games like football that may exclude some children due to preconceptions or past experiences!
- Be brief with your instructions and get to the point so they can start the game!
- Be enthusiastic and get involved – you are the best role model.
- Get creative – you don't need expensive equipment to set up physical games like the 'human knot'.

Advantages

- Physical games can build self-esteem if everyone is included. Emphasize that physical activity should be enjoyment over competition!
- The children can improve aerobic capacity, flexibility and muscle strength.
- You don't need a lot of time and space to include physical games in the daily routine!
- Physical games are a fantastic way to motivate boys and can be used to develop communication, language and literacy skills!

Adaptations

Get the children to involve their parents/carers in devising a list of physical games they played.

Use it as a behavioural reward – you get to choose the 'game of the day' if you have demonstrated a desired behaviour.

Integrate physical games into other areas of learning, for example 'Men in Boats'. Hoops are scattered around the floor, children 'swim' around the floor space until 'Men in Boats' is shouted with a number or sum for the children to solve; the resulting number of children have to get into the hoop/boat – it is great in promoting mental maths!

Questions for Consideration

How good a role model are you in terms of physical games? Do you get involved and wear the appropriate clothing when leading physical games?

How do you encourage the more 'reluctant' members of your group to get involved?

Linked Resources

Setting Routines – See page 63
Outdoor Area – See page 64

Resource:	'Activate to Concentrate'

Explanation

The thinking behind *Activate to Concentrate* is simple – young children have an inbuilt need and desire to be 'up and doing and moving'. Sometimes this 'need' can result in behavioural difficulties, particularly if the practitioner/teacher is trying to work with a group of children or is trying to teach the class when the children are wriggling, fidgeting, restless and inattentive. A quick burst of *Activate to Concentrate* time can help children to shake off some of their excess energy which will then help them to refocus and concentrate on their learning. A couple of minutes of star jumps, running on the spot, trunk twists, marching, stretches, hopping on the spot and/or sprints is all that is needed to help children become attentive and listen to you.

Handy Hints

- Gather together upbeat songs which you can play during *Activate to Concentrate* time so that there is a steady beat/pulse to which you and the children can perform the different activities.
- If there are health and safety concerns of performing *Activate to Concentrate* activities indoors, utilize the space you have in the outdoor play area/playground.
- Consider doing some *Activate to Concentrate* activities *before* your setting opens in the morning – might you be able to encourage some of your children's parents/carers to join in?
- Create a simple pamphlet about *Activate to Concentrate* so that parents and carers understand why you are doing lots of bursts of energetic activity with the children throughout the session/day.

Advantages

- Children are highly motivated by *Activate to Concentrate* activities.
- Using short bursts of energetic activity really helps to alleviate behavioural difficulties in the setting.
- *Activate to Concentrate* activities help to keep children active and healthy.
- Research has shown that *Activate to Concentrate* activities have a positive impact on children's attainment levels and their ability to focus on their learning.

Adaptations

For younger children or those with physical disabilities, select *Activate to Concentrate* activities which require a limited amount of co-ordination – some children will not be able to perform movements in unison so consider using running, jumping and dancing activities to start with.

For older children, develop a number of routines which can be led by small groups of children so that *you* can activate to concentrate!

Questions for Consideration

Do you know of any settings in your local area which use *Activate to Concentrate* activities to engage their children? Might you plan to go and see these in action to ascertain their effectiveness?

Where is there a good space in your setting to engage in *Activate to Concentrate* activities?

Linked Resources

Physical Games – See page 89
Dance – See page 88

Resource:	'Diet' (Helen Wilson)

Explanation

What a child eats and drinks, i.e. their diet, can and does have an effect on their behaviour. There has been a great deal of research into the impact that different foods have on the way children behave. Young children grow and learn at an amazing rate. In order to have the energy required to grow, move and learn, young children need a balanced diet of nourishing food and plenty of water. A varied diet will provide all the different proteins, carbohydrates, fats, vitamins and minerals a young child needs. A good diet can also improve concentration and energy levels, thereby increasing children's learning potential.

Handy Hints

- Set a good example by eating healthy yourself.
- Involve children in food shopping, choices and preparation.
- Get all the staff involved in creating or reviewing the healthy-eating policy within the setting as this involvement helps all staff in the setting to understand the objective of a healthy-eating approach and to appreciate the reasons why snacks and meal times are run as they are.
- When introducing children to new foods, it is important that they have the chance to try the same food on more than one occasion. The first time they try a food, they may reject it but this can be because it is a new flavour or they do not like the texture, colour or smell of the food.
- Do not let food become a means of reward or punishment.

Advantages

- If children see others, particularly role models, eating new and unusual foods, they will feel it is safe to try the food themselves.
- Snack times and lunchtime are fantastic opportunities to develop language. Children's talk does not have to be about the food; general chit-chat about their play and their homes is very valuable too. It is amazing what you can find out about children's lives when you have time to sit and listen.

Adaptations

To see how much water a child is drinking, when a child has had a drink they could put their name on a board or put a picture of a water droplet next to their name/photo. The adults can do this too!

Some children may not have had breakfast so consider offering a breakfast table until 9.30 in the mornings, with small bowls of cereal and cartons of milk so that the children can help themselves.

Playing is the main way children learn and this is no different when learning about food – children need time to explore and play with different foods.

Questions for Consideration

Do you and your staff act as positive role models and eat healthy foods alongside the children?

Consider this … We need to be careful about how we talk about food as no food should be labelled 'bad'; it is about creating an understanding of what makes a balanced, healthy diet that is important.

Linked Resources

Your Behaviour – See page 8
Parents/Carers – See page 47

Resource:	'Places of Worship'

Explanation

An exciting way to make religion and faith come alive for children is to take them on an educational visit to a place of worship, e.g. a church, mosque, synagogue, etc. Visits of this nature can be a powerful way of helping to promote positive behaviours in the children you work with when they are there, e.g. listening behaviours, walking behaviours, politeness and being calm/reflective. These visits also help children to appreciate that people behave in different ways when they are in a place of worship as this is considered appropriate within the particular context, e.g. holding their hands in the air, bowing, meditating, etc. Visits can help to promote exploratory behaviours in children and it is not unusual for these places of worship to fire their curiosity; you will find that children will ask a lot of questions because they are engaged and interested!

Handy Hints

- Always have a good ratio of adults to children to ensure that behavioural difficulties do not occur as a result of not having enough adult supervision to keep your children under control.
- Model the behaviours you want your children to emulate so that they understand what is expected of them, e.g. move slowly and quietly; use a low, respectful voice; and listen attentively to the person who is showing you and the children around the place of worship.
- Regularly remind children of your expectations in terms of behaviour and reward those who meet your expectations; use non-verbal strategies – see Referee Cards (page 33) and Behaviour Binoculars (page 30) for ideas to 'warn' children of any behaviours they exhibit which you deem to be undesirable or inappropriate.

Advantages

- Places of worship can help to promote tolerance in children as they begin to appreciate how different people live their lives.
- The promotion and application of positive behaviours can be made *prior* to the visit, *during* and *after* the visit.
- Places of worship are designed to encourage people to be calm and respectful; many practitioners/teachers are keen to promote these behaviours in the children they work with.

Adaptations

For very young children (0–3), visits to places of worship may not be appropriate. Consider inviting a member of the faith community to come to your setting or speak to them prior to a visit to establish age quotas.

For older children, encourage them to demonstrate inquiry behaviours by making a note of questions they would like the answer to before they visit; following the visit, reflect on what they discovered and ascertain if they have found out what they wanted to know.

Questions for Consideration

When was the last time that you took the children you work with to a place of worship?

What specific behaviours would you like to promote when you take your children to a place of worship? Why?

Linked Resources

Sensory Areas – See page 69
Assemblies – See page 78

Resource:	'Constructive Criticism'

Explanation

While no one particularly likes receiving constructive criticism, it is important to remember that this can be an effective way to develop positive behaviours in the children that you work with. For some children, constructive criticism is necessary to make them aware of the undesirable behaviours they are exhibiting; it is important for them to understand the effect that these behaviours are having on their learning, the other children's learning in the setting, and your ability to teach them. Many practitioners/teachers are not keen on being critical about children in their setting but it is important to remember that young children have an in-built resilience and do 'bounce back' quite quickly with support and encouragement from you, other staff members in the setting, and their parents/carers.

Handy Hints

- Ensure that the criticism you give relates to the behaviour and not the child, e.g. *'Claire, I like you, but I am unhappy when you do not listen to me when we are on the carpet'*.
- Consider when is the best time to give the criticism to the child – individually? In front of their peers? At the end of the session/day with their parents/carers? Consider the outcome of this and the impact you are hoping to have by giving it in this particular way.
- Help children to realize that their behaviour will improve if you work together by setting little targets for them to achieve, e.g. putting up their hand when answering a question; sitting close to the practitioner/ teacher on the carpet; sitting away from their friends so that they are not distracted when they are working.

Advantages

- Constructive criticism can get right to the heart of the issue so that the child knows exactly what they are doing which you deem to be inappropriate/undesirable.
- Protecting the self-esteem of the child helps to maintain positive relationships between you and the children in your setting.
- Short, specific targets help to give children a clear direction as to how they can make necessary improvements to their behaviour.

Adaptations

For younger children, think carefully about the language that you use with them so that they are not confused by what you say.

For children with special educational needs, ensure that the criticism is focused on one particular behaviour which can be easily targeted and addressed.

For older children, consider sharing your criticism in writing with them, encouraging them to note down two ways in which they intend to address your concerns.

Questions for Consideration

Which children do you think would respond positively to constructive criticism in your setting? Why?

How long will you give children to address their inappropriate behaviour – 10 minutes? An hour? A day? Why so?

Linked Resources

Instructions – See page 94
Behaviour Targets – See page 55

Resource:	'Instructions'

Explanation

We use instructions to help us assemble furniture, find places, cook food and for many other everyday activities. Sometimes, without these instructions, we would find it challenging to complete tasks. Children have an equally difficult time coping without instructions or goals and this can result in poor behaviour. Instructions for children need to be specific; you need to make sure the instructions communicate to the children exactly what you want them to do. Keep the instructions concise; if they are too complex, the children will find it difficult to follow them.

With good guidance, children are less likely to present bad behaviour and are aware that they need to complete a specific task that has been assigned to them – instructions keep children on task.

Handy Hints

- Only introduce the instructions for one activity or job initially and then gradually introduce the children to instructions for other aspects of learning or setting routines.
- Ensure children have visual prompts to support them in following the instructions.
- Ask the children if the instructions are easy to follow; if not, adapt them with the children's support.
- Give the children an opportunity to decide what they need instructions for in the setting – is there anything that they are unsure of or that they think would be easier to do with guidance?
- Work with the practitioner/teacher the children will be with during the next academic year, and to make the transition easier, offer them the instructions the children are already aware of.
- Only use one-step instructions to keep them simple and easy to follow.

Advantages

- The children can complete tasks independently by following instructions.
- You can use the instructions for any activity/task.
- The children are able to work more independently – as a result, they feel in control of what they are doing and trusted.
- Using instructions can save you time in the long run.
- The instructions become routine for the children.

Adaptations

Ask the children to help you decide on the instructions you write. Depending on the age of the children, they can sit with you or attempt to write the instructions independently. This activity involves the children in the strategy and also develops their instructional, speaking and listening, and writing skills.

Use a photographic slide show or PowerPoint presentation to display the instructions on the interactive whiteboard.

Questions for Consideration

How many instructions do you think you should use for each task/role in order for the children to be able to follow them without getting confused?

How would you display instructions in your setting?

Linked Resource

Setting Routines – See page 63

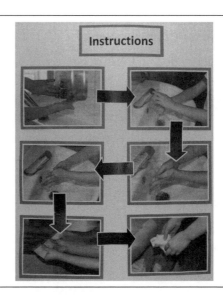

9

Reflective Resources

Resource:	'Rules/Essential Agreements'

Explanation

At the beginning of a term with a new class or group of children, it is important to establish a set of agreements or rules for a setting. The most effective way to do this is to involve the children as the rules/agreements will then be more relevant to them and so the children will be more likely to follow them. Children need expectations and will feel respected and valued if they are included in decisions about what is expected of them.

The idea of an agreement should be introduced to the children in a way that involves them – for example, ask them to think of things it is important to do in order to make the practitioner/teacher happy. Use this list to create a set of agreements by supporting the children in phrasing the behavioural expectations for their setting.

Handy Hints

- Ensure the rules/agreements are positive – start them with 'We will' or 'I can'. Using a negative opener can impact on the children's attitude towards the agreements.
- Display the rules/agreements clearly in the classroom.
- Ask the children to sign their names against the rules/agreements, laminate this sheet and display it on the wall next to the rules. If the children happen to break any of the rules/agreements, remind them that they agreed to follow the rules/agreements and show them their names.
- Use the word 'agreement' rather than 'rule' with younger children as it is more child-friendly.
- If an incident does arise in the classroom, refer to the rules/agreements and ask the children to tell you which one they need to remember.
- Support and gently guide the children when they are deciding the rules/agreements but do not set them yourself.

Advantages

- The children are involved in the rules/agreements and so have a stronger desire to follow them.
- The rules/agreements are clearly visible and easy to refer to as a reminder to set clear expectations for the children.
- Because the rules/agreements are decided from the beginning of the year, the children become familiar with them and begin to refer to them without prompting.

Adaptations

Involve the children in supporting the strategy by asking them to recognize those respecting the rules/agreements with stickers or praise.

You could ask the children to write/decide upon a set of playground/outdoor agreements and assign monitors to support others if any problems arise during outdoor playtimes.

For younger children, you could use photographs to model the agreements rather than text.

Questions for Consideration

How would you introduce the idea of a set of rules/agreements to the children in your setting?

Where in your setting would be a good place to display the agreements?

Linked Resources

Setting Routines – See page 63
Behaviour Targets – See page 55

Essential Agreement

We will be polite, kind and will share with our classmates

We will care for each other

We will take care of everything in our classroom

Resource:	'Thinking Chair'

Case Study

Sam, aged 6, had deliberately scribbled on another child's work on a whiteboard whilst sitting on the carpet during whole-class work. The teaching assistant took Sam and sat him on the 'thinking chair', where she then explained that Sam needed to think about what had happened. The teaching assistant set an electronic timer for 5 minutes and left it with Sam. At the end of the 5 minutes, the teaching assistant returned to the child and asked him to explain why he had been placed on the thinking chair. Sam described what he had done and was then prompted to consider why this behaviour was inappropriate. Following this, the teacher spoke to Sam and asked him what should happen now. Sam thought that he should apologise to the child and try to help the other child to write out the answers again on his whiteboard. The teaching assistant then praised Sam for his successful thinking time and monitored him while he carried out his agreement.

Handy Hints

- Use the thinking chair to manage minor behavioural issues.
- Consider the location of the chair in your setting, making sure the child can still be seen.
- Use a sand/electronic timer to ensure the child is not forgotten.
- If the child is missing any work, ensure they complete the work in their own time.
- Ensure that a dialogue takes place following the thinking time period.
- Do not keep the children on the 'thinking chair' for an excessive amount of time – a maximum of 5 minutes is appropriate.
- Reflect on positive things the child has done as an example of behaviours you like and have seen from them. Always end discussions with the child with a positive comment.

Advantages

- There is time available for both you and the child to calm down before discussing the behavioural incident.
- Less intrusion on teaching time is assured. The children can take time out and you can work with them without interrupting your teaching.
- The child is given an opportunity to think about their actions.
- It involves the children in managing their own behaviour if the reflection, following their time on the thinking chair is carried out.

Adaptations

You may consider a similar approach with older children, perhaps using an area in the classroom rather than a specific chair. Encourage the children to be involved in the time-out area by perhaps asking them to sit there if they feel they need to. Approach the children after a couple of minutes and carry out a discussion to establish and resolve any issues.

WARNING: Some children may use the time-out area as a personal break, so establish a set of expectations for its use.

Questions for Consideration

What would you do if you were teaching a PE lesson outside and felt you needed to use the thinking chair?

How will you incorporate the thinking chair into the behavioural strategies you are currently using?

Linked Resource

Calming Cushions – See page 98

Resource:	'Calming Cushions'

Explanation

Calming cushions are a great way of helping children to release their feelings of anger and frustration in a safe and supportive way. Sometimes children get so frustrated that dealing with their emotions in a calm and rational way is not possible; as opposed to letting children kick and punch others to 'get it out of their system', calming cushions help children to compose themselves after a safe 'release' of their emotions. The cushions are simply normal cushions which children can use to squeeze, pull, twist, punch, wrestle with or 'drop kick' so that they can exert their feelings without causing harm to another person. Once the child has had a chance to calm down, they can then return to their activities effectively.

Handy Hints

- Consider where you might allow the children to 'use' the cushions – letting other children watch as a child has an 'aggressive release' is not appropriate.
- Calming cushions should not be used by all children, every day. They need to be kept in a special place (in a box or in a cupboard) so that children appreciate they are not part of the 'furniture' of the setting.
- Let frustrated children explore the cushion in their own way – this is not a resource which necessarily needs to be modelled to the children by practitioners/teachers.
- Ask the children how they feel once they have 'used' the cushion – you will find that children feel a lot better after using it.

Advantages

- Calming cushions are a relatively cheap resource to purchase and use in your setting.
- Calming cushions allow children to express their physical emotions in a safe way.
- The release that children feel from 'using' the cushions helps children to appreciate the importance of expressing strong emotions.

Adaptations

Alternatives to the calming cushions include stress balls, plastercine, Blu-Tack®, stretchy slime and balls of wool.

For older children, practitioners/teachers can let children handle the calming cushions as they talk to them about their feelings.

Children with special educational needs and disabilities can be encouraged to handle and 'use' sensory cushions.

Questions for Consideration

Which children in your setting struggle to deal effectively with their strong emotions?

When particularly do you think calming cushions would be useful during the day – *after playtime? At the end of a lesson/session?* Why?

Linked Resources

Anger Management – See page 68
Physical Games – See page 89

Resource:	'Rest Mats'

Explanation

This is an idea which we have taken from practice observed in the United States. At certain periods during the session/day, the practitioner/teacher tells the children that it is 'Rest Time'. In response to this, the children in the setting stop what they are doing and collect their own personal mat (a yoga type mat), find a space on the floor and lie on their mat, either to sleep, reflect, shut their eyes or consider what they are going to do next. The children are taught that this is not a time for talking or interacting with others; it is a time where children can 'rest' their brains for a little while. After a period of time, the practitioner/teacher lets the children know that 'Rest Time' is over; the children then jump up, clear away their mats and get back to their learning.

Handy Hints

- Ensure that the mats are clearly marked so that each child knows which mat belongs to them – different colours, shapes and labels might help.
- Initially demonstrate the behaviours you expect of the children so that they have a clear idea of what they should be doing on the mat.
- Praise children who are demonstrating the behaviours you want to see when the children are on the mats; quietly speak to children who are not behaving appropriately or use your effective non-verbal strategies (see Chapter 1 for further ideas).

Advantages

- This strategy gives both you and the children 'time to breathe'; in essence it is an effective 'Time Out' for both of you.
- Giving the brain periods of rest helps children to be more focused and effective when they are actually working with you; see this strategy as a way of promoting good learning and teaching conditions.
- 'Rest Time' is a good strategy to use when the children in your setting are unnecessarily noisy (when it is windy) or when they become overly excited, for example when it is Christmas or near to long holiday periods.

Adaptations

This could be renamed as 'Down Time', 'Time Out', 'Chill Time' or 'Reflection Time' depending on the age of the children.

For older children, encourage them to self-evaluate their behaviour – have they been well behaved? How do they know? What could they do to be even better behaved?

As opposed to staying in the setting, consider taking the children into the outdoor play area, the playground or the hall.

Questions for Consideration

What are the cost implications for you in buying mats for all the children in your setting?

Are there space implications which may hinder you being able to fully realize/implement this strategy?

What would you do if a child falls into a deep sleep during 'Rest Time'?

Linked Resources

Calming Cushions – See page 98
Sand Timers – See page 103

Resource:	'Star of the Week'

Explanation

At the end of every week, a child who has shown outstanding behaviour, effort or achievement is chosen by their class teacher/practitioner as a 'Star of the Week'. The child is recognized in a weekly assembly if in a school or at a set time in a nursery/PVI setting, and the reason for them being chosen is read out. The child may be given a sticker or certificate to acknowledge their achievement, which will allow them to share their success with their parents/carers.

Handy Hints

- Photograph the children who are the stars, and if your setting/school website is password-protected you can upload their photographs weekly to the year group/home page.
- Give the children a certificate to take home to show their parents that they were the star this week.
- Emphasize how special being the star of the week is to the other children, and encourage them to show their peers recognition/respect. This makes the award even more special.
- Make sure that there is room on the certificate for you to write the reason why the child was the star so that it reinforces the positive behaviour.
- Record the names of the children who have been given the star of the week so that you can look for reasons to give all children in the class an award over the year.

Advantages

- It is a very specific and individual recognition of good work or behaviour.
- The children are recognized by all if the certificates are presented at an assembly or when all children are gathered together.
- The children's parents are involved in the strategy as a certificate will go home as part of the reward.
- It is a positive end to a week for the children, and is something to work towards.
- It is inexpensive and easy to resource.

Adaptations

The same idea could be used in a PVI setting/ foundation unit. The children's photographs could be displayed on the wall with the reason for them being the star of the week, rather than the presentation being done in an assembly. The children could also still take home a certificate so they can share their success with their parents/carers.

Older children may not enjoy the certificate aspect of this reward and may prefer a more informal recognition, for example credits or a free-time pass.

Questions for Consideration

What would you do if a child was particularly shy and reluctant to stand up in assembly to receive their certificate?

Who do you think should present the children with their certificates?

Linked Resources

Special Helper Role – See page 17
Certificates – See page 60
End of Term/Year Awards Assembly – See page 81

Resource:	'Make-Me-Smile Board'

Explanation

The Make-Me-Smile Board is an A3 laminated piece of yellow card with a large smiley face drawn in the middle of it. The Board should be used at the start of every session/day; the children should be asked what they could do, in terms of their behaviour, to make you, the practitioner/teacher 'smile', e.g. work hard, be kind to others, hold the door open for someone, push all the chairs under the tables, or switch the lights off in the setting at playtime. When individuals actually demonstrate these behaviours, the practitioner/teacher (or the children themselves) should write the child's name on the board. At the end of the session/day, the practitioner/teacher should review the names on the board, highlighting why these names are on the board and offer praise for the behaviours they have exhibited. These children are then eligible to either have a treat or gather their coats and line up first for dinner/home time.

Handy Hints

- Make sure the Make-Me-Smile Board is nice and big so that all of the children in the setting can see it. In our settings, we have all used a large smiley face but we have known colleagues who have taken a photograph of themselves smiling and enlarged this onto the board.
- Have small pieces of paper to hand so that if you are away from the Make-Me-Smile Board you can make a record of the child's name who has made you smile; you can then ask that child to Blu-Tack® their name onto the board. When you bring the children together at the end of a session/day, this is an ideal time to make the rest of the children aware of those who have made you smile.
- Show children your smile when you raise awareness to their good behaviour – children respond very positively to this.

Advantages

- This simple resource promotes the 'positives' in children's behaviour and acknowledges those who are behaving well.
- It can be adapted and used with any age group of children.
- The Make-Me-Smile Board can respond to the expectations of all practitioners/teachers, settings and their policies.
- Most children like to please their practitioner/teacher and so will respond positively to this strategy.

Adaptations

For younger children, it is good to specify which behaviours you like to see that make you smile. These behaviours could be ones that you are particularly targeting in your setting, e.g. turn taking behaviours, honesty, sharing and listening behaviours.

For older children, the board can be 'operated' by Make-Me-Smile Monitors which maintain the upkeep and use of the board in class – this promotes positive behaviours, especially if the children have to make their peers smile!

Questions for Consideration

Which behaviours would you actively promote through the use of the Make-Me-Smile Board with the children in your setting?

What reward would you give for a child who gets their name on the board five times in a row?

Linked Resources

Star of the Week – See page 100
Rules/Essential Agreements – See page 96

Resource:	'Traffic Lights'

Case Study

It was Monday morning and Mr Cottle found that some of the children in his class were very unsettled. Oscar was being quite silly during carpet time so Mr Cottle looked through the names sitting around the outside of the traffic lights and moved Oscar's name to the amber light, which is equal to a verbal warning. Oscar stopped for a short time but then began to disrupt the other children; Mr Cottle then moved him to the red traffic light whilst continuing to teach the other children. Oscar recognized his mistake and sat sensibly. After the session, Mr Cottle spoke to Oscar and explained that if he had continued to make bad choices there would have been a consequence. He asked Oscar to explain what would have happened if his behaviour had continued. Oscar told Mr Cottle that he knew if he had made another bad choice he would have gone for time out in another classroom.

Handy Hints

- You can use photographs of the children to accompany names for younger children.
- When a child has had a time out, allow them to start at the beginning of the strategy again.
- Make sure the strategy is always easily accessible so that if you are working with children you do not need to disrupt activities to move a child's name.
- If you are working in an open setting, keep the traffic lights portable so that you can take them with you.
- Speak to the colleague you will send children to for time out when you need to use a sanction; they may not appreciate a child arriving without any prior knowledge.

Advantages

- This is a strategy that allows management in teaching time with minimal disruptions.
- You can support the children to encourage those whose names are on the green light, as peer recognition is also a powerful reward strategy.
- It is a very visual strategy which the children are easily able to follow.
- All children are familiar with traffic lights and so easily identify with the strategy.

Adaptations

Why not modify the system so that instead of using red, amber and green lights, you try:

- multiple thumbs up, single thumb up, single thumb down,
- sunshine, sun and cloud, rain cloud
- grinning face, happy face, sad face.

If you are working in a setting for SEN with partially sighted children, you could use a selection of sounds or short bursts of music to represent the traffic lights as you call names.

You could use the interactive whiteboard to make a set of traffic lights.

Questions for Consideration

How will you take a reward to the next level after a child has been on the green traffic light and continues to model good behaviour?

Would you allow a child to move back to the beginning of the strategy if they had taken time out in another class?

Linked Resources

Referee Cards – See page 33
Stop and Go Cards – See page 35

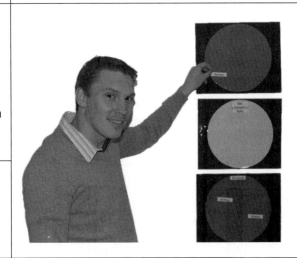

Resource:	'Sand Timers' (Helen Wilson)

Explanation

Sand timers are a visual way of measuring time. They consist of two glass or plastic bulbs placed on top of each other connected by a narrow tube which when turned upside down allow the coloured sand to flow from one bulb to another. They can measure 1-, 2-, 3-, 5-, 10-, 15- and even 30-minute intervals. Sand timers are a fantastic resource that can be used very successfully in early years settings to help with, for example, turn taking on the computer and getting dressed more quickly after a games session, times on bikes and other popular activities.

Handy Hints

- Sand timers can be used to promote concentration and positive behaviour.
- Use a particular sand timer for quick starters and finishers – you have 1 minute to get your things out or you have 3 minutes to finish the sentence you are writing!
- Sand timers on individuals' desks are great for targeting particular desired behaviours.
- Mix rewards with an attainable target; for example, keeping on task in silence for 1 minute gets a reward stamp on a chart.
- Sand timers can be used to get quiet from the whole class. Hold up the 30-second timer as a signal for silence – anyone still talking after the timer has run through does not get a reward.

Advantages

- Sand timers are a very visual method of measuring time that is accessible to all children.
- Sand timers can be used in a whole host of situations.
- Sand timers can be used with other reward systems to promote positive behaviours.
- Children love using them and being in control of turning over the timer!

Adaptations

Egg timers can be used to effectively measure time.

Smart Notebook and *Active Studio* have a great timer that will count up or down as requested. They are very visual with an audible 'beeper' when the designated time is up. Timers can be enlarged to fill the whole screen if necessary for a particular task.

Timers are great to introduce competitiveness into tasks – for example which group can put away all the equipment the most, quickly and the quietest?

Sand timers can be used for whole-class, group or individual tasks.

Questions for Consideration

Have you considered getting the children to set themselves their own time targets for particular activities to give them more ownership of their behaviours?

Have you ever considered using a sand timer to develop concentration or to promote healthy competition?

Linked Resources

Positive Praise – See page 12
Stickers – See page 52
Reward Charts – See page 110
Stamps – See page 36

Resource:	'Noise-O-Meter'

Explanation

The Noise-O-Meter is a simple resource which helps to control the noise level of children in your setting. It is made up of a piece of semi-circular shaped card that is split into three 'pizza' shaped pieces – one green, one yellow and one red. A blue arrow is attached to the card so that it can pivot and point to each colour. The green part of the Noise-O-Meter indicates that the noise level in the setting is good. However, if the arrow is moved to the yellow part, then the noise level is getting a little too loud and the children in the setting need to lower their voices. If the arrow is moved to point to the red part, then this means that the noise level is unacceptable and the children must calm their voices immediately. A change in the noise level results in a swing of the arrow back to yellow and ultimately green.

Handy Hints

- Always have the arrow pointing to green when the children come into the setting – start a session on a positive! However, if the children do come in noisily, it is only right to show them how their noise does not merit a green marker on the Noise-O-Meter scale.
- If you move the arrow to the yellow or red part of the Noise-O-Meter, always ask the children to explain why they think you have moved it there.
- As soon as you notice some improvement in the noise level of the children, then move the arrow back towards the green.
- If you want to manage the noise volume of a group of children, then make a smaller version of the Noise-O-Meter just for them; ensure that this is displayed close by to where they are working.

Advantages

- This resource is a great way of controlling noise levels without you having to raise your voice.
- The Noise-O-Meter is a good way of supporting children's understanding of the importance of colour, i.e. traffic lights, referee cards.
- The resource can be very easily made.
- Children respond very quickly to the resource, particularly if you highlight the change in the reading to one child; they will very quickly pass on the message to the other children for you!

Adaptations

For younger children, you might only want to have the green and yellow parts on your Noise-O-Meter to make it easier for them to understand.

For older children, you might include percentages around the edge of the Noise-O-Meter to promote mathematical readings of scales.

Parents and carers can easily use this strategy at home to manage the noise levels of children at home.

Questions for Consideration

Would you want your Noise-O-Meter to be operated by the children or just by yourself? Why so?

What size would you make your Noise-O-Meter? What difference do you think the size would make if using this with individuals/120 pupils?

Linked Resources

10cm Ruler – See page 32
Whistle or Bell – See page 31

Resource:	'Tremendous Teddy'

Explanation

Every early years classroom will have a collection of teddy bears, dolls and stuffed toys. There is usually one toy, however, which is loved by all of the children in the setting; in one of our settings it was Tremendous Teddy. The idea behind Tremendous Teddy is that he can only be petted or handled by children who are well behaved; every child has a chance to cuddle him and 'take him for little walks' but the children have to show the practitioner/teacher and the rest of the group/class 'brilliant behaviours' which Teddy shares with the practitioner/teacher in their ear through little growls. Those who Teddy sees as modelling these 'brilliant behaviours' from his chair/basket are allowed to care for him.

Handy Hints

- Encourage children to believe that Teddy is alive by using your dramatic skills and puppetry techniques.
- Strive to make Teddy special by creating a special place for him in the setting, e.g. on a special chair or in a small basket.
- Carefully consider which behaviours you want Teddy to promote as 'brilliant behaviours' *before* he growls at you!
- Decide whether you will use Teddy every day or once during the week as a strategy for promoting 'brilliant behaviours' with the children you work with.

Advantages

- Children love the idea of caring for an animal – if you show that Teddy is a special bear, the children will work harder to show him their 'brilliant behaviours'.
- Children really believe in Teddy if you convince them that he is important to you.
- Every setting has a toy which practitioners could use as Teddy.
- Parents can use this idea to help manage their child's behaviour at home.

Adaptations

For younger children, a hand puppet is useful so that you can create movement and emotions out of the character.

For older children, a real animal, e.g. a hamster or a small rabbit, can act as a real substitute for Teddy – many settings are purchasing real animals to promote caring behaviours in children.

Questions for Consideration

What toy do you have in your setting which you could use as Teddy – why have you selected this one?

What 'brilliant behaviours' might you get *your* Teddy to promote in your classroom/group?

Linked Resources

Wow Card – See page 34
Star of the Week – See page 100

10

Rewarding Good Behaviour

Resource:	'Individual Reward Schemes'

Explanation

Children who are not responding to whole-class management techniques may need a more personalized scheme to follow. It may be that the child has specific needs or that they are simply going through a 'bad patch'. Children are unique and, as a result, will respond to rewards and behaviour strategies in different ways. It is important that practitioners/teachers find out about children in their setting who require an individual reward chart so that the strategy they create will engage and motivate the child to make the best choices about the way they behave.

Handy Hints

- Try not to use the same strategy for more than one child unless the children request the same strategy. Re-using a strategy can make it less appealing for some children.
- Do not have too many children on individual reward charts at any one time. If there are lots of children to monitor, it may become unmanageable.
- Be creative – don't feel that you have to use stickers all the time – why not try the following ideas: gems in a jar, marbles in a bowl, adding petals to a flower, adding teeth to a crocodile's mouth, or moving a character up a ladder.
- When children have achieved a pre-agreed number of stickers, teeth on a crocodile, etc., allow them to have a small reward which could be a certificate or a small gift.

Advantages

- The children are being recognized as individuals and will respond to this as well as to the reward scheme itself.
- Other children can be involved and support children who have a chart.
- This strategy involves parents/carers as it can be easily used at home. Using the strategy at home will also reinforce the child's understanding of how it works and how they should be behaving.
- The reward schemes are easy to initiate and can be relatively cost-free.

Adaptations

Allow the child to choose the reward scheme they will follow. Offer the children a selection based on your interpretation of suitable strategies and ask them to find one they would like to use. By allowing the child to be so involved they have more interest in the strategy and are more likely to respond positively to it.

Encourage other children to notice children with a chart making good choices and sharing with you when they do.

Questions for Consideration

How would you make sure the child with an individual reward scheme was properly supported away from the classroom?

Can you think of adults in your setting who could support you in monitoring children with individual reward schemes?

Linked Resources

Reward Charts – See page 110
Stickers – See page 52
One-to-One Time – See page 77

Resource:	'Afternoon Tea with the Head Teacher'

Case Study

It was Friday morning at Whistlestop Primary School, and the children were sat in assembly waiting anxiously. Mrs Harton stood at the front of the assembly and rummaged through a bag full of tokens. She picked out six tokens and called out the names written on them to the whole school. Children cheered as they heard their names, while others groaned as they realized they had missed out that week.

That same afternoon, the children whose names were picked went to have afternoon tea with the head and to play games and chat while other children in class desperately tried to earn tokens for the next week's draw.

NB: As the children receive their tokens, their names are written on the back of them so that when the tokens are drawn at the end of each week, everyone who has received a token has a chance.

Handy Hints

- Let the children be involved in planning what they will be eating for afternoon tea and setting it up.
- Plan games for the children to play when they have had their afternoon tea with the setting manager/head teacher.
- Give older children a question and answer time with the setting manager/head teacher.
- Don't give the children potentially stimulating, fizzy or sugary drinks. Their practitioner/teacher will not thank you when they return to their setting.
- Allow the children to be involved in the draw of tokens/tickets – this role can be assigned to the child who had the most tokens at the last draw but whose token was not drawn.

Advantages

- The children respond well to incentives and this is a very exclusive treat.
- The setting manager/head teacher is recognized for rewarding and not just for disciplining children.
- The setting manager/head teacher has an opportunity to get to know the children on a social level.
- The draw can be an exciting part of the week for all children who have received a token.

Adaptations

Older children would probably rather not sit with their head teacher for afternoon tea. Why not allow them to suggest a favourite teacher that they would like to spend time with? The head teacher could support this by covering the chosen teacher's class, allowing for this to happen.

You could walk the children to a local cafe instead of having afternoon tea in the setting itself.

Questions for Consideration

While afternoon tea with the head is very exciting, could you arrange for someone else to come into school to have tea with the children as an end-of-term treat? Who might that be?

How many children would attend the afternoon tea each time?

Linked Resources

Raffle Tickets – See page 38
End of Term/Year Awards Assembly – See page 81
Places of Worship – See page 92

Resource:	'Free Choice'

Explanation

One of the most effective ways of rewarding children for their good behaviour is by giving them 'free choice' with regards to the toys that they play with or the activities that they engage with. There are always particular resources that children like to get out, e.g. Bee Bots, the special football, the felt tip pens (!), and activities such as playing on the computer, going on the climbing frame or asking the practitioner/teacher '20 questions'. All of these activities excite and motivate children – by knowing what these resources and activities are, you can offer them to children as part of their 'free choice' of activities when they have completed set tasks.

Handy Hints

- To make it manageable, ensure that you establish six resources and six activities which the children can select from as part of their 'free choice', otherwise it may become difficult to manage what all of the children decide to use and do; this could cause behavioural difficulties!
- Ensure that these 'free choice' resources and activities are readily available so that children can maximize their time engaging with them (do ensure there is adequate time for them to get involved in them as well!).
- Plan for these resources and activities to be used/undertaken *throughout each day* as opposed to always being on a Friday afternoon; if a child has to wait until Friday afternoon for their 'free choice' activity and they are ill that day, what was the incentive of them behaving well Monday through to Thursday?

Advantages

- If children have something that *they* want to play with/do, then they are more likely to behave well and try hard with their learning as opposed to playing with resources or doing activities which the practitioner/teacher perceives as being enjoyable for children.
- Resources and activities can be changed frequently to respond to the needs and interests of the children you work with.
- Practitioners/teachers will see a 'different side' to the children they work with when they see their children engaged in something *they* want to do.

Adaptations

For younger children, plan for regular periods throughout the day so that children do not have to 'wait' for their reward of free choice at the end of the session/day/week.

For older children, consider allowing individuals to select activities which groups of children/the whole class can engage in.

Encourage parents and carers to use free choice as a reward for good behaviour at home.

Questions for Consideration

What activities do you think the children you work with would choose for 'free choice'? What do you think might be influencing their choice?

What implications are there on time/money/space/location/resources with the 'free choices' that children make? How will you manage these?

Linked Resources

TV/DVD Time – See page 116
Individual Reward Schemes – See page 107

Resource:	'Reward Charts' (Helen Wilson)

Explanation

A reward chart is simply a daily or weekly chart devised to capture positive behaviour as and when it happens. All children like to know what they have done well and the reward chart is a very simple but powerful way of recording positive behaviour. You can stick stickers on, ink stamp or simply colour in sections of a chart as a reward for a positive behaviour. It is a very visible way of showing just how well a child is progressing in terms of positive behaviour. It also allows you to focus and recognize when a child is doing something well rather than concentrating solely on the negative behaviours. They are very simple to design yourself or there are a multitude of designs that can be bought based on favourite themes.

Handy Hints

- Your motivation is the key to making these reward charts a success – don't use them half-heartedly and do get the child involved from the beginning.
- Choose one positive behaviour to concentrate on rewarding.
- Always remember to reward the positive behaviour immediately to get maximum effect.
- Make sure everyone is involved and is giving consistent praise and reward for specific behaviours.
- Make sure the chart is visible to both the child and adults so that they have the maximum impact.
- Be consistent in rewarding positive behaviours.

Advantages

- A reward chart is a simple and easy-to-manage method of focusing on positive behaviours that everyone can be involved in.
- It highlights the positive behaviours, not the negative ones.
- Reward charts are very flexible and can be adapted for use in any situation.
- The chart teaches the child the importance of delayed gratification – they have to work towards their final reward.

Adaptations

You can use reward charts to promote a variety of positive behaviours, including active listening, saying 'please' and 'thank you', sharing and helping to tidy up.

Reward charts can be used for groups of children to promote a particular positive behaviour, for example putting books away carefully.

You can vary the format to make the chart thematic and more relevant to the particular child or group of children – you could design a friendship tree with each leaf being a reward for an act of kindness, or an octopus with each sucker on its tentacle being a reward.

Questions for Consideration

Would a reward chart work for all children? You must really get to know what works for individual children in order to achieve a change in behaviour.

Have you involved all staff and parents who come into contact with the child in the setting in using the reward chart system?

Linked Resources

Positive Praise – See page 12
Stamps – See page 36
Stickers – See page 52
Teaching Assistants – See page 41

Resource:	'Special Privileges'

Explanation

Every practitioner/teacher knows that children like to receive rewards for their good work and behaviour. One way in which children can be rewarded is through special privileges – activities, duties and 'jobs' for a select few. These can be used as and when it is deemed appropriate, and can come in a variety of different forms, e.g. being first in the line to the dinner hall; taking the register to the school secretary; sitting on the chair next to the lead practitioner/teacher; holding the practitioner's/teacher's hand as the child leads the rest of the class into the hall for assembly; switching off the lights in the setting at the end of the session/lesson – children *love* these kinds of privileges, particularly if you encourage children to see them as 'special' and 'important'.

Handy Hints

- Work with your TA/colleagues to identify different privileges that you will use in your setting.
- Keep a record of who earns which privileges so that they are shared out evenly among all of the children.
- Think about how regularly you intend to use these different privileges with the children – will they lose their impact if you use them all of the time?
- Consider discussing with the children what privileges *they* would like to work towards – they are more likely to strive to attain them if they have some say in what they are.
- Display the privileges in the setting so that children are reminded of what privileges are on offer.

Advantages

- Children like being given 'special jobs' to do – it validates them and makes them feel good about themselves.
- While special privileges might seem like simple things to practitioners/teachers, they are meaningful and important to children.
- Children feel a sense of achievement when they are given a special privilege; once they receive one, they will work hard to earn another one.

Adaptations

Place older children in groups and get them to talk about the kinds of privileges they consider to be 'special' or 'important' in the classroom – you may be surprised at what they consider to be 'special'!

With younger children, make them feel important by offering verbal praise for being the 'special' sweeper-upper or the only child to be allowed to sit on the practitioner's/teacher's chair.

Questions for Consideration

Do you already use special privileges in your setting? Do they work? If so, why? If not, why not?

Are there privileges which you could offer to children which could help the day run smoothly? Such as Register monitor? Milk monitor? Cloakroom monitor?

Linked Resources

Individual Reward Schemes – See page 107
Free Choice – See page 109

Resource:	'House Points/Table Points'

Explanation

The idea behind this strategy is that the children work together within their 'houses' or with their table groups to earn points. The children can earn points in a variety of ways; you can tailor the requirements in order to manage specific behaviour in your setting. The children could be given points for raising their hands, tidying their table, doing good collaborative work, following instructions, or remaining on task and doing great work. At the end of a week, half term or term, the scores are tallied for each table or house and depending on what you have decided, at the beginning of the week, half term or term, the winning group/house will win a group prize or reward.

Handy Hints

- Display the weekly house/table points on a board in the classroom so that the children can see how they are doing – this will encourage a little healthy competition and motivation in the setting.
- Refer to the points to remind children about expectations before starting an activity.
- Remind the children that they are working as part of a team to encourage collaborative work.
- Re-cap the reasons why the children received points; this will remind the children of your expectations.
- Occasionally award an individual with a point for the whole table; this child will be recognized by their classmates and children will try to model the behaviour as they will be keen to receive the same recognition.
- With table points, you could offer the children a week of staying indoors at playtime.

Advantages

- The children work together either for their house or their table.
- It is an accumulative reward strategy that gives both immediate and long-term recognition.
- Children are aware of your expectations.
- You can change the rewards easily; children will be excited to see what they receive!
- You can bring maths into this strategy. The children can learn to use tally charts and you could even invite some children to collate the results and make a bar chart to display at the end of a term or week.

Adaptations

The house points can be collated as a school and each house can be rewarded together when the points are tallied. This can be done by giving all children in the house a party, an extra playtime or a small gift.

You could encourage the children to collect class points and to compete against other classes in the setting. You could tally the points at an end-of-term assembly.

Questions for Consideration

Do you have houses in your setting? If not, could you introduce them? What would you call the houses?

Could you involve the children in choosing the rewards? How would you do this?

What behaviours would you look for from table groups?

Linked Resource

End of Term/Year Awards Assembly – See page 81

Resource:	'Whole-class Reward Schemes'

Explanation

The children are given a way to 'earn' points or credits as a class or group; when they reach a certain number of points or credits they receive a reward. You can establish with the children how they earn these points in a discussion. It is, however, important that all the children are involved. The following are examples of possible behaviours the children might undertake to receive a point/credit: great tidying up, being sensible while moving around the setting, good collaboration, taking care of property in the setting or great whole-class listening. Every time the children work together and achieve any of the agreed criteria; they receive a reward or a token towards a treat.

It is for you and your children to decide what the reward should be. Here are some suggestions: parachute time, extra play, class party, watching a movie, sports, games, choosing time, free computer time or baking.

Handy Hints

- Allow the children to be a part of choosing the reward.
- 'Gimme 5' is a great way to encourage the children to stop what they are doing and to listen to your instructions. As you call 'Gimme 5', the children simply put down what they are doing, stop talking, look to you and put their hands in the air. If the children *all* stop when you call 'Gimme 5', it might be a good opportunity to give them a point/credit.
- Perhaps explain to the children when rewards will be given – it might be an idea to assign an afternoon rather than a morning session. If the children have choosing time on a Monday morning, it may prove difficult to refocus them!
- Record the points/credits on a chart in your setting so the children can see how many they need to get to receive the reward.

Advantages

- By encouraging the children to work together, they build a camaraderie that will enhance any group work done in your setting.
- The children will enjoy the rewards together.
- The rewards can be fun for you to enjoy as well as for the children.
- You can vary the types of credits given and the rewards the children receive which means that this strategy is likely to remain effective.

Adaptations

Depending on your setting, you may want to group the children. If you have a large open setting then the rewards may come around very quickly and be difficult to manage and arrange. By putting the children into reward groups, these problems can be overcome.

Invite older children to develop the criteria for receiving a point/credit and assign someone to keep track of the scores.

Questions for Consideration

For what reasons will your give points/credits in your setting?

What rewards will you offer the children in your setting?

How many points/credits will the children need to collect to get a reward?

Linked Resources

House Points/Table Points – See page 112
Lining-up Award – See page 114

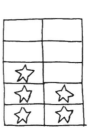

Resource:	'Lining-up Award'

Explanation

From a very young age, children in educational settings are expected to line up for various reasons, including for lunch, assembly and to move to new activities. Lining up and moving in a line is not an easy thing for children to do – often arguments and scuffles break out as children chat and move. To support the children in making the right choices when forming a line, you can introduce a positive reward strategy as an incentive to encourage the children. At the end of each lunch hour, playtime or assembly, introduce an award for the group of children who make the best line. The award might be a trophy, medal or mascot. Reinforce the strategy by encouraging the children to support others when their group is lining up, modelling good behaviour.

Handy Hints

- Assign children to be line monitors to head the front and back of the lines and to model to other children how to line up.
- Put up a lining-up award chart with each group/class's name on the wall in your setting. Add a 'trophy' or 'star' every time to the group of children who make the best line.
- Try to have an adult at the front and back of the line (with the monitors) to support the children in moving to their destinations sensibly.
- Ask the children to decide on a set of expectations for lining up so they know what you expect of them.
- Call table groups or houses one at a time to line up so that the children do not all rush at once.

Advantages

- The children learn to move more sensibly and quietly around a setting.
- The children find the element of competition with other children in the setting fun.
- The children are working together to achieve, so the strategy builds a supportive relationship among them.
- Soon lining up sensibly becomes second nature and the children require less prompting.

Adaptations

Older children could judge the younger classes or nursery groups to decide on who gets the award.

You may extend the lining-up award to include moving to destinations. Often children find moving as a group quite challenging, so by setting expectations and extending the reward you can support the children in managing their behaviour.

Line up all the children from every group in the setting for fun once a week, and score the children on how well they do.

Questions for Consideration

What would you do to recognize the children who receive the lining-up award at the end of a week?

Who would judge the award in your setting?

Linked Resources

Whole-class Reward Schemes – See page 113
House Points/Table Points – See page 112

Resource:	'Extra Playtime' (Helen Wilson)

Explanation

Extra playtime is a very simple, free and very effective resource! 'Playtime' is anytime outside structured activity time – it does not have to be outside and it can be integrated into normal activity time or at natural breaks in the day, both indoors or outside. Extra playtime can be given as a reward for positive behaviour for individuals or groups of children. It is an opportunity to allow children to choose their favourite activity and to have extra time engaging with it. It is a very effective resource for use with children of all ages!

Handy Hints

- 'Extra playtime' can be used as an impromptu reward for a particular positive behaviour on the spot or it can be built into the next session or even next day's planning for maximum effect if time is short.
- Always check with the individual child what extra playtime would be most desired. Do not assume that all children would like more time outside. Some hate being outside!
- Do not overuse the reward as overuse can lessen the impact!
- Never 'take back' the extra playtime as punishment, as it was given as a reward for a different and positive behaviour. Use another sanction to deal with the unwanted behaviour.
- Involve all staff in using the reward, through all aspects of the school day to reinforce the consistency of behavioural expectations.

Advantages

- It is a free resource that can be tailor-made to meet every individual's needs.
- It allows you to see what children enjoy and dislike doing in terms of activities.
- If used occasionally, the 'extra playtime' can be a special reward for exceptional behaviour or a reward for a completed reward chart.

Adaptations

You can get a child or a group of children to plan all the activities with you for a session.

You could reward different positive behaviours with specific time allocations so the children can choose to redeem their 'time points' straight away or save them up until the end of the week. Sand timers would be a good way of demonstrating what the periods of time represent.

Questions for Consideration

Are you aware of what play activities the children in your setting like and dislike? Make sure you let them choose – do not choose for them!

Does your planning allow flexibility for you to be able to commit time for individuals to have extra playtime? It should!

Linked Resources

Teaching Assistants – See page 41
Learning Mentors – See page 42
Midday Supervisors – See page 43

Resource:	'TV/DVD Time'

Explanation

Of the children we have collectively taught, the one reward they all love is 'TV Time'. The use of a television with either a DVD or video can have a real effect on children's behaviour, particularly if the whole group/class have to work together to earn minutes for TV time which can be built up over the day/week. The use of TVs can be a useful teaching resource, in terms of educating children through educational programmes. TV Time can also be a real motivator for children to behave, particularly when individuals have a *choice* of what they would like to watch (from the selection of *appropriate* videos/DVDs you have on offer).

Handy Hints

- Avoid always having TV Time on a Friday afternoon – mix it up sometimes so that children can have TV Time on a Tuesday morning as a surprise.
- If children in your setting like a particular character, e.g. Postman Pat/the Tweenies, ensure that you have a selection of episodes for them to choose from. Ensure you have permission to show these DVDs/videos in public.
- Take care with playing DVDs and videos with a PG rating.
- Encourage children to bring in videos and DVDs they would like to play from home – ensure that they are not full-length films but short, 10–15 minute episodes of programmes they like to watch.

Advantages	**Adaptations**
<ul><li>TV Time is a great way to reward the children in your setting for their good behaviour.</li><li>TV Time gives all children in your setting something to work towards in terms of behaving well – if you display the video/DVD case of the programme that the children might be watching at the start of the week, children are more likely to behave well if they know what their reward is going to be.</li><li>TV Time is a useful way of developing children's attention and concentration skills; these are positive behaviours that children need to develop as they grow up.</li></ul>	For older children, they could save the minutes they earn for TV Time over a number of weeks so that they can watch a 25-minute programme instead of a short, 10-minute episode. TV Time can be used as a valuable learning tool if the practitioner/teacher has watched the programme prior to the children seeing it – if the practitioner/teacher sets particular questions which the children get right after the 'showing', they could earn more minutes!

Questions for Consideration

What programmes do your children like to watch? How do you know this?

Where might you be able to get episodes from the shows that your children like?

Are there any programmes/characters which you will not let the children watch? Why?

Linked Resources

Reward Charts – See page 110
Whole-class Reward Schemes – See page 113

Appendices

Behavioural Observation Recording Sheet 1

Start time	End time	Child	Age	Initials of observer		Comments
Activity				**Setting**	**Behaviour**	**Incidents**

	Consequences

Now refer to page 120 for 'things to consider' before selecting a strategy.

Photocopiable:

A Quick Guide to Behaviour Management in the Early Years © Emily Bullock and Simon Brownhill, 2011 (SAGE)

Behavioural Observation Recording Sheet 2

Name _____

Date / /

Observation carried out by _____

	8.30–9.00	9.00–10.00	10.00–11.00	11.00–12.00	12.00–1.00	1.00–2.00	2.00–3.00	3.00–3.30
Behaviours Humming loudly Behaving disruptively Calling out Being aggressive Using bad language Refusing to participate								
Antecedent Told 'no' Told 'wait' Asked to move away Asked to do an activity Not working with friends Does not like activity Has home issues								
Consequences Asked to take time out Given a warning Given attention Removed from the setting Behaviour chart used Behaviour ignored								

Collate the scores and then refer to page 120 for 'things to consider' before selecting a strategy.

Photocopiable:

A Quick Guide to Behaviour Management in the Early Years © Emily Bullock and Simon Brownhill, 2011 (SAGE)

Behavioural Observation Recording Sheet 3

Child's Name _____

Carpet Time Assessment

Behaviours	2 mins	4 mins	6 mins	8 mins	10 mins	12 mins	14 mins	16 mins
Touching other children								
Calling out								
Fiddling with clothing								
Talking to peers								
Being aggressive towards others								
Crawling around the carpet area								
Swearing								
Total Scores								

Simply tick in the boxes every time the child presents one of the behaviours for each time increment of a session. Collate the scores and then refer to page 120 for 'things to consider' before selecting a strategy.

Consider This

When reviewing the behavioural observations, consider the following before you take action:

- At what time of day do the incidents occur?

- Who is around the child when incidents occur?

- At what frequency does the behaviour occur? Is there only one type of behaviour that is repeating itself?

- Where does the behaviour occur?

- Is there a day of the week that more incidents occur?

- What do you think the child is trying to communicate?

- Has the child had support previously? If yes, what form of support has the child responded to in the past?

- Have colleagues who have worked with the child got any useful information that might support you in managing their behaviour?

- Could you speak to the child's family and discuss incidents that may have happened at home to affect the child's behaviour in the setting?

- If the family has not experienced any issues at home, can the family offer any ideas or strategies that they use at home?

- Are there any issues at home that you are aware of that parents/carers are not willing to divulge?

- Is this a one-off incident or is the child regularly involved in behavioural incidents?

- Is your relationship with the child good – maybe ask for a colleague's opinion?

- Is the child challenged by the work in your setting?

- Does the child find the work too challenging?

- Does the child respond better to child-initiated activities or teacher-led activities?

- How does the child respond socially to others in the setting?

Now having considered these points, look at the chapters and browse strategies that you feel may work for the child you have observed.

Effectiveness Rating Sheet for Strategies

Strategy	Page Number	Effectiveness Rating	Comment
		/10	
		/10	
		/10	
		/10	
		/10	
		/10	

References

Cowley, S. (2010) *Getting the Buggers to Behave*, 4th edn. London: Continuum.

Department for Children, Schools and Families (DCSF) (2008a) *Statutory Framework for the Early Years Foundation Stage*. London: DCSF.

Department for Children, Schools and Families (DCSF) (2008b) *The Independent Review of the Primary Curriculum*. Available at: www.education.gov.uk/publications/ standard/publicationdetail/page1/BLNK-01010-2008. London: DCSF.

Dix, P. (2010) *The Essential Guide to Taking Care of Behaviour*. Harlow: Pearson.

Gardner, H. (2006) *Multiple Intelligences: New Horizons in Theory and Practice*. New York: Basic Books.

Hardin, C.J. (2004) *Effective Classroom Management: Models and Strategies for Today's Classrooms*. Columbus, OH: Merrill Prentice Hall.

Maslow, A.H. (1943) 'A Theory of Human Motivation', *Psychological Review* 50(4): 370–96.

Ofsted (2006) *Improving Behaviour*. London: Ofsted.

Piaget, J. (1951) *The Psychology of Intelligence*. London: Routledge.

Rogers, B. and McPherson, E. (2008) *Behaviour Management with Young Children*. London: Sage.

Shelton, F. and Brownhill, S. (2008) *Effective Behaviour Management in the Primary Classroom*. Maidenhead: Open University Press.

Van der Veer, R. and Valsiner, J. (1991) *Understanding Vygotsky: A Quest for Synthesis*. Oxford: Basil Blackwell.

Index

Page numbers in bold refer to topics dealt within in detail.